Foreword: Ro

IDOLS RIOT!

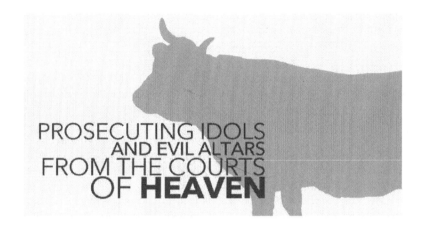

PROSECUTING IDOLS
AND EVIL ALTARS
FROM THE COURTS
OF **HEAVEN**

By

Katie Souza
Dr. Francis Myles

"Includes Powerful Prayers of Activation!"

This product is available at special quantity discounts for bulk purchase for sales promotions, premiums, fund-raising, and educational needs. For details, call us at (602) 888-0364 or visit our websites at www.francismyles.com or www.katiesouza.com

Idols Riot by Katie Souza & Dr. Francis Myles
Published by Katie Souza Ministries & Francis Myles International
1776 N Scottsdale Rd, Unit 2467, Scottsdale, Arizona 85252

Visit the authors' websites at katiesouza.com or francismyles.com
Library of Congress Cataloging-in-Publication Data:
An application to register this book for cataloging has been submitted to the Library of Congress.
International Standard Book Number:
E-book ISBN:
Printed in the United States of America

Table of Contents

Foreword

As I began to understand the Courts of Heaven, my whole perspective of the spirit realm changed. Whereas I had always been a *prayer warrior* that felt if something wasn't moving or answers weren't coming, it must have been because I hadn't prayed or functioned long enough or hard enough. This is what I had been taught, or at least was the implication I had believed. As I came to see the Court of Heaven, this changed. I began to understand that I wasn't trying to convince God to do something for me through prayer. I was operating in a covenant position with Him to see things rearranged in the spirit world. I realized that things were legal in the spirit realm, and therefore I had to undo legal cases the devil was using to resist me. This would allow heaven to be manifested in the earth. Of course, this is what Jesus taught us to pray in Matthew 6: 9-10.

In this manner, therefore, pray: Our Father in heaven, Hallowed be Your name. Your kingdom come. Your will be done, On earth as it is in heaven.

We are here to see the passion and deep desire of the Lord brought into reality in the earth. One of the chief ways this is done is by presenting cases in the Courts of Heaven that allows God as Judge the right to render decisions to allow this to happen. The Bible is clear that God operates and functions as the ultimate Judge. Hebrews 12:23 states this with great clarity.

… to the general assembly and church of the firstborn who are registered in heaven, to God the Judge of all, to the spirits of just men made perfect,

When you read this scripture in context, you realize that we have been granted access to come before the Lord as Judge. Part of our inheritance and purpose is to undo Satan's legal claims by presenting cases before the Lord as Judge, based on what Jesus has done for us. According to Isaiah 54:17, voices, tongues, and words against us in the spirit world can be silenced.

No weapon formed against you shall prosper, And every tongue which rises against you in judgment You shall condemn. This is the heritage of the servants of the Lord, And their righteousness is from Me," Says the Lord.

Notice that it is the *tongue* that rises against us that we bring into condemnation. The real key to undoing the rights of the devil against us is to silence the different voices that are speaking. We do this through the blood of Jesus. Hebrews 12:24 lets us know that the blood of Jesus is speaking better things than that of Abel, who cried for vengeance against Cain for killing him.

… to Jesus the Mediator of the new covenant, and to the blood of sprinkling that speaks better things than that of Abel.

With the blood of Jesus and the covenant He made with us through it, we can silence every voice. Any voice that is claiming a legal right against us because it *owns* us due to ignorant or known activities with demonic powers in our ancestry can be silenced. Their rights to curse us, devour us, and even destroy us are revoked and removed. Dr. Francis Myles and Katie Souza do such an astounding job in this book,

Idols Riot, to help us walk out this process. They teach us how to prosecute these things in the Court of Heaven and see their rights revoked from determining our destiny and future!

In our natural judicial systems, a judge cannot render a verdict without a petition or evidence being presented. He cannot judge or do something because He wants to. This is our job in the Courts of Heaven. We are to come before God as Judge and present our case on behalf of ourselves, others, or the assignments God has given us. Often, the lack of answers coming from our efforts in prayer is because there hasn't been an adequate case presented to allow God as Judge to render decisions for us. A true story I was told helps demonstrate this necessary concept.

There was a young lawyer representing his client in a court case in a natural court setting. This lawyer was beginning his presentation of facts, evidence, and testimony. As he spoke before the judge, he begins to ramble on and on. The judge sat patiently and listened. However, after a while, the judge finally said, *"Young man, please stop."* The young attorney did what the judge requested. The judge then said, *"I know what you are trying to do, but you're going to have to give me a reason."* This is such a revealing idea that we must embrace. The judge knew what the young attorney desired. He understood the verdict and the decision he wanted. He even *wanted* to grant it to him.

However, the evidence and/or the way it was presented was insufficient to allow him to do this. This is what happens with us before the heavenly court if we haven't been instructed in these matters. How often have we rambled on and on before God as Judge, but never made our case? He, as the judge, knows what we are requesting, and as our Father, also wants to grant us our petition. We, however, have not made our case. In this book, *Idols Riot,* we are taught how to do this. We will no longer be flailing in the spirit realm seeking to be sufficient. We will be able to make our case clear, see the Lord as Judge receive it, and experience the breakthroughs that come from decisions rendered on our behalf. This book is a game-changer for many. May you see the cry of your heart answered from the Courts of Heaven.

Robert Henderson
Best-Selling Author, *Court of Heaven Series*

Preface

But seek first the kingdom of God and His righteousness, and all these things shall be added to you. 34 Therefore do not worry about tomorrow, for tomorrow will worry about its own things. Sufficient for the day is its own trouble.

Matthew 6:33 (NKJV)

৵৵৵

JESUS SETS the plumb line from which God triangulates all of His dealings with His creation, both celestial and terrestrial. This divine plumb line is an unmovable line, an ancient landmark, so to speak. It's an uncompromising standard of righteousness for both right and successful living in God's Kingdom. This righteous standard is an eternal order! It's a "spiritual order of things" that both defines and determines who is approved or disapproved of God! I call this eternal "order" the *"Order of First Things!"* Through this eternal order, we quickly come to terms with this exciting and chilling truth, ***"God demands first place, every time, everywhere, from everyone or none at all!"*** Prayerfully meditate on this statement and let this sacred and unchanging truth sink into your spirit!

In the sixth chapter of Matthew's gospel, Jesus makes a very compelling case as to why most humans, including people of faith, are plagued with endless worries about the basic necessities of life! Because God and the demands of His Kingdom do not yet occupy an "unchallenged first place" position in their life! For many so-called

Bible-believing Christians, once you get past their self-righteous lip service to God, you see that God is not first in their life! Without beating about the bush, Jesus admonishes us to *seek **first** the Kingdom of God and His righteousness, and all these things shall be added to us*. Take note that the primary emphasis of Jesus in the above passage hinges on the word, "First!"

Our Proton God!

But I have this [one charge to make] against you: that you have left (abandoned) the love that you had at first [you have deserted Me, your first love].

Revelation 2:4 (AMPC)

"Seek ye first" is a command to stop idolizing anything that God never intended to occupy such a lofty and sacred position. "First," determines what you love and follow! "First" also determines and defines what you value the most! "First," predicts what you will hold on to when everything else around you is falling apart! "First" also signifies what you are willing to die for! Most importantly, "First" *reveals what you truly worship, and if it's not God, you have just discovered your idol!*

The Greek word for "First" is "Prōton." A "proton" is a subatomic particle found in the nucleus of every atom, which carries a positive charge. However, in Greek linguistics, the word "prōton" also refers to "something preeminent, in both rank and importance." According to Thayer's and Strong's Greek Lexicon, prōton has the following meanings:

1. First in time or place
2. First in any succession of things or persons
3. First in rank
4. First in influence, or honor
5. Chief
6. Principal
7. First, at the first

When you examine this word, "prōton," it was as though God was thinking about His relationship to all of His creatures when He designed the prōton inside the atom. The message is loud and clear! God wants to be the prōton inside everything we say or do! This book is about dethroning idols and the altars we have erected to these idols in our soul so that God has no competition of any kind! Ask yourself this question: *"Is the LORD, my prōton God, or does He come in at second place to the idols in my heart?"* Selah!

The Principle of Pre-Eminence!

[Now] He is the exact likeness of the unseen God [the visible representation of the invisible]; He is the Firstborn of all creation. [16] For it was in Him that all things were created, in heaven and on earth, things seen and things unseen, whether thrones, dominions, rulers, or authorities; all things were created and exist through Him [by His service, intervention] and in and for Him. [17] And He Himself existed before all things, and in Him all things consist (cohere, are held together). [18] He also is the Head of [His] body, the church; seeing He is the Beginning, the Firstborn from among the

dead, so that He alone in everything and in every respect might occupy the chief place [stand first and be preeminent].

Colossians 1:15-18

Examining the majestic beauty of the "prōton" we are brought right into the heart of the *"order of first things!"* We finally dive into what the "order of first things" entails and contains. The "order of first things" entails returning to the LORD, His rightful place and role as His Eminence! By definition, the word "eminence" means " a high station, rank, or reputation." In the English language, the suffix "Pre or Re" is not a word by itself. It is meant to convey the idea of returning anything to its original state before it was compromised or moved.

The "order of first things" also contains "persons, things, principles, concepts and doctrines" that hold preeminence over all other truths in both heaven and earth. When you have to choose between God and your idol, God should be your first choice, as He occupies a place of preeminence among all other gods (which are not really gods, but demon spirits). When you have a conflict between the Word of God and the educated opinions of men (no matter how many PhDs they have), the Word of God holds preeminence.

When you are faced with choosing between Yeshua-Jesus and any other cultural Messiah, whether it's Muhammed or Buddha, you must choose Jesus or be eternally lost! Why? According to Acts 4:11-12, *"This [Jesus] is the Stone which was despised and rejected by you, the builders, but which has become the Head of the corner [the Cornerstone]. [12] And there is salvation in and through no one else, for there is no other name under heaven given among men by and in which we must be saved."* This is how, and why, knowing the "order of first things" will help us make wise and godly decisions.

Consequences of Violating the Order of First Things

Samuel said, Has the Lord as great a delight in burnt offerings and sacrifices as in obeying the voice of the Lord? Behold, to obey is better than sacrifice, and to hearken than the fat of rams. [23] For rebellion is as the sin of witchcraft, and stubbornness is as idolatry and teraphim (household good luck images). Because you have rejected the word of the Lord, He also has rejected you from being king.

1 Samuel 15:22-23

The Bible contains many biblical case studies of the dire and tragic spiritual consequences of violating the order of first things! The tragic stories of men such as King Saul, King Solomon, and Judas Iscariot quickly comes to mind. The violation of this eternal order, or divine plumbline, often results in the following:

- Abortion of our God-given purpose
- Hijacking of destinies
- Defeat before our enemies
- Loss of life, relationships, resources, status, and time

This book "Idols Riot" will show you how to avoid the pitfalls that occur when we violate this eternal order of first things. I pray that it will save you much future heartache and help prevent you from falling into the traps of the enemy as the above-mentioned kings. Most importantly, this book contains the spiritual protocol for how to enter the "Courts of Heaven" and prosecute "idols and evil altars" in your bloodline that Satan has been using to cause you to "violate the order of first things."

Yours for His Kingdom,

Dr. Francis Myles
Co-author: *Idols Riot!*

1

Idols: Breaking the First Commandment

by

Katie Souza

You shall have no other gods before or besides Me. [4] *You shall not make yourself any graven image [to worship it] or any likeness of anything that is in the heavens above, or that is in the earth beneath, or that is in the water under the earth;* [5] *You shall not bow down yourself to them or serve them; for I the Lord your God am a jealous God, visiting the iniquity of the fathers upon the children to the third and fourth generation of those who hate Me.*

Exodus 20:3-5

GOD COMMANDS US to put Him first, and according to scripture, the biggest thing that comes against His commandment is idolatry. *What are idols? In biblical terms, an "idol is anything (person or thing) that you place (give first place to) above God!"* Idols can be anything or anyone that has captured your thoughts more than Jesus has. If you spend more time thinking and talking about your beloved sports, a new electronic device, or the hottest music star or movie actor, you have probably made those things or people into an idol. Idols are also things that, in many different ways, will steal from you. Most notably, idols are *time* stealers who always go after your secret place with the Lord. They control you and drive you to spend more time with them than Him. If game day has turned into an everyday event whose time outweighs your worship in your prayer closet, then you are standing on dangerous ground.

Likewise, idols will steal your money by luring you to buy a bigger home that you can't steward effectively. Sometimes idols will lure you into getting the latest luxury car you can't afford to maintain. They also push you to overspend on items such as home goods, clothing, and face products that end up unused under the sink. Each dollar you spend is spent in the hope that the products' promise of satisfaction will be true.

However, after you acquire the costly things, you discover they fail miserably at fulfilling you. As a result, you are off again on another hunt for something else to magically achieve your soulish need for satisfaction. Soon you find yourself repeating this cycle over and over again while spending more money and energy, each time only to be disappointed.

Idols are any person or thing you place above God.

Before you say, "Katie, idols are an Old Testament subject. We are under grace and not under the law." Let me quickly point out this warning in the New Testament from the Apostle John in 1 John 5:21. *"Little children, keep yourselves from idols (false gods)—[from anything and everything that would occupy the place in your heart due to God, from any sort of substitute for Him that would take first place in your life]* (AMPC)." For those who still think that a message on idols is Old Testament, how do you explain that the Apostle John wrote his epistle to

New Testament saints who lived under the same dispensation of grace that we live under today? Today's church is "worshipping" idols more than ever! The day the Holy Spirit tells you that He has searched you and found "no idols" is the day you should take the biggest praise break of your life! But until then, please consume the contents of this book with the intensity of a drowning man grasping for a lifeline.

Unfortunately, the Body of Christ has no idea how much these idols are affecting, destroying, and shipwrecking our lives today. I will give you one shocking example. I have a friend by the name of John Blake. I love him and his wife, Ana, dearly. Both of them were faithful employees of mine of over ten years. During that time, John suffered from a lot of different illnesses. One of his ailments caused him to exhibit symptoms like Alzheimer's. He would forget basic skills like how to type. After he would watch a movie, he couldn't remember any of the plot. He often was unable to complete sentences, so his wife would jump in and complete them for him. When John went to sleep, he would enter into a coma-like sleep, from which you couldn't wake him up. It was quite scary, to say the least. As a result, he was put on 15 different medications costing him 1500 dollars a month to stop him from slipping into a coma!

When doctors tested John, they found out that he did not have Alzheimer's, but rather an unusual disease where excessive levels of ammonia were being stored up in his brain. All human beings have ammonia in their bodies in small amounts because it helps us to process our food and also aids other functions in the body. However, when the levels of ammonia get too high, it can become dangerously toxic, as in John's case. That's what was causing John to exhibit these Alzheimer's-like symptoms. During the years John suffered in this condition, he received a lot of prayer with no success whatsoever! It was pure hell for him and his wife.

One day, one of my staff members had a prophetic dream that led to John's deliverance. In the dream, this staffer could smell ammonia. I then looked up the word "ammonia," and what I found was shocking. Ammonia comes from the Greek word "Amonikos, or Amon," because ammonia was first obtained from a region near the temple of the god Amon in Libya and Egypt. Amon was one of the many gods the Egyptians worshiped. When I realized that the word "ammonia" was derived from an Egyptian idol, I thought to myself, "Wow, I wonder if this has anything to do with John's condition?" When I went to sleep that night, I had a confirming dream. In the dream, I could also smell ammonia. When I woke up, I was convinced. I thought, "Wow, John's got something on his brain, and it has to do with this Egyptian god." That day I went into the office and told John what happened. Then I invited him over to my house so we could pray for him. For an hour, I laid hands on him, worshipped, and prayed that his soul would be healed (we will talk about this later). When our time with the Lord was completed, John got up and instantly recognized that his mind was clear, more than it had been for years.

Then John left my place and went home. For his whole life, he had always smelled ammonia whenever he showered. So much so, he thought it was normal for everyone. However, that night after I prayed for him to be delivered from the idol in his soul, he got in the shower and suddenly realized that he smelled no "ammonia" coming off his body. Then over the following days, he noticed that his memory was coming back rapidly. He no longer couldn't finish his sentences. He could remember the movies he watched and even gained back his ability to type. Thrilled, he now was convinced something supernatural had happened to him. So, he decided to ask three of his doctors to test his ammonia levels independently. When the tests came back, for the first time, his ammonia levels were perfectly normal!

Idols are Deaf, Dumb, Blind, and Crippled

"And served their idols, which were a snare to them. ^{37} *Yes, they sacrificed their sons and their daughters to demons."*

Psalm 106:36-37 (AMPC)

The Bible states that when the Israelites worshipped idols, they were placing their lives in the hands of evil spirits that these ancient statues represented. Idols are really demon spirits. It is critical that you understand this fact: when you make anything into an idol, you are inviting a demonic spirit to get involved with you. Hello, I hope you caught that! When you make anything into an idol, including your children or spouse, you are inviting a demonic spirit to attack you! What are these idols able to do? Actually, the list would be shorter if I told you what they cannot do. Let me give you some examples.

The Bible says idols are **deaf, dumb, blind, and crippled**. In Psalm 135:16, it says, "Idols have mouths, but they speak not; eyes they have, but they see not." The book of Revelation 9:20 says that "the people did not stop worshiping demons, their idols of gold, silver, bronze, stone, and wood, idols that cannot see, hear or walk." What does this mean, and how does it affect you? First of all, it means that since all idols can't "see, hear, speak or walk," they can make you have these kinds of issues in your physical body. According to the law of worship, "you become like what you worship!" Do you know why so many miracles of blind-eyes opening, deaf-ears opening, the mute speaking, and the lame walking happen overseas? It is because, in most third world countries, many of their cultures are open to the public worship of idols. So, when a miracle-worker like myself preaches the gospel of Jesus in these nations and the people forsake their idols to serve the living God, the miracles described above follow naturally!

Since idols cannot speak, they can cause you to have muttering and stuttering in your speech. I remember the first time I saw a demon spirit that caused people to have speech problems and be mute. It had scaly reptilian skin grown over its mouth so it could not speak.

Idols can also cause deafness and other hearing issues such as ear infections, tinnitus, and ringing, just to name a few. Mark 9 and Matthew 17 contains the story of Jesus casting a deaf and dumb spirit out of a child. How did that poor boy get to be in that condition? Thayer's lexicon says this about the word "dumb" (Greek alalos) *"speechless, dumb, lacking the faculty of speech: because the defects of demoniacs were thought to proceed from the nature and peculiarities of the demons by which they were possessed."* Did you see that? This child was both deaf and dumb because he was displaying the characteristics of the demon that possessed him. What kind of demon was it? I believe it was a spirit behind an ancient idol. According to Matthew 17, this child was also epileptic or "moonstruck." The moon goddess was one of the most commonly worshipped idols in ancient times. Even today, the moon is worshipped by many, and its cycles are used to help witches, warlocks, and sorcerers cast evil spells over people to gain more authority over them.

Many times, idols are also behind blindness and other issues with vision such as dry eye, floaters, and cataracts. Case in point, the story in Mark 10:46-52 of Blind Bartimaeus. The Bible tells us that before Jesus healed him, he sat in the streets of Jerusalem, begging for his existence because he was blind. After the LORD gave me the revelation on idols, I suddenly noticed something in the story that I had never seen before. The Bible goes out of its way to emphasize that he was called "blind Bartimaeus, son of Timaeus." I wondered why the Bible went out of its way to tell us who Bartimaeus' father was. The Bible does not identify the parentage of many of the people who got healed by Jesus. So I believe scripture highlights this because of what the name "Timaeus" means. It means "to defile oneself with idols."

Idols have mouths, but they speak not, eyes they have, but they see not.

Wow! Bartimaeus' father was into idolatry. So much so, he had not only defiled himself with his worship of these idols but also corrupted his family. Don't forget the Bible says that idols cannot see and again that the ancients believed that the physical defects of demoniacs were a direct result of the nature and peculiarities of the demons by which they were possessed. I believe the idols in Bartimaeus' life caused him to lose his eyesight. I see a lot of eye miracles in my meetings when I teach about idols and how to get rid of them. It's normal for blurry vision to clear up, cataracts to dissolve immediately, and people who had floaters their entire lives to be healed.

Idols can also cause you to be crippled in your physical body and to suffer from various diseases like rheumatoid arthritis, scoliosis, and other skeletal and muscular issues. Think about it, since the Bible says idols cannot walk, having idols in your life gives Satan the legal right to cause you to be crippled in your body. There is a biblical example of this in Acts 14. It says there was a man in Lystra, "who couldn't use his feet, he was a cripple from birth." However, as he sat listening to the Apostle Paul's preaching, he received faith to be healed. Paul, recognizing this, shouted for him to stand up on his feet, and the man leaped and walked! The response from the surrounding crowd was shocking! Look at what they did.

> *"And the crowds, when they saw what Paul had done, lifted up their voices, shouting in the Lycaonian language, the gods have come down to us in human form! 12 They called Barnabas Zeus, and they called Paul, because he led in the discourse, Hermes [god of speech]. 13 And the priest of Zeus, whose [temple] was at the entrance of the town, brought bulls and garlands to the [city's] gates and wanted to join the people in offering sacrifice."*
>
> Acts 14:11-13

Wow! Lystra was a city dedicated to worshipping idols! So much so, the people thought Paul and Barnabas were the gods they worshipped coming down to earth to perform miracles. The citizens of Lystra, along with their priest, a worshipper of the demon god Jupiter, wanted to bring sacrifices to Paul and Barnabas! That is what they would typically ***do for their demon gods!*** No wonder that poor man had been born crippled in his feet. Idolatry ran in his bloodline. Idols can't walk; thus, the people that worship them display those same characteristics.

Idols are why many people in our world are walking around with canes and are stuck to wheelchairs. I'll give you an example of this kind of miracle happening in the USA. At one of my events, a man named Gunther had a crippling disease. He told me that he had come to my meeting wearing two orthopedic braces on both knees and walking with a cane. The reason was that nine months prior, he woke up and couldn't put any weight on his left knee. Finally, he was forced to go to an orthopedic surgeon, who said his femur was fracturing but didn't know why. Shortly after, his right knee went out, fracturing both his femur and tibia. When the doctor ordered an MRI, he discovered that his bones had disintegrated to such an extent they were fracturing and breaking. In fact, both femurs and the right tibia looked like spider webs, and the doctors could not diagnose why it was happening. The doctors said he was not even a good prospect for knee replacements, because if the bones kept fracturing, the replacements wouldn't hold.

Thankfully, that night during one of my meetings, I had a word of knowledge about knees being healed, and Gunther immediately received it by faith. The next day, he told me that he had to walk a block to his car after the meeting, still wearing his orthopedic supports, but had no pain. At that point, he believed the Lord had healed him. That same night he took off both braces and put the cane aside, and for the first time in nine months, he had no pain. Before the miracle, the pain was so excruciating at times that on a scale 0 to 10, it was a 12 or 13!

The morning after, Gunther came up on the stage to testify about his miracle! He was still not wearing his braces. He came up the stairs with no cane and with no problems. He even did some squats to demonstrate his miracle. Something the doctors had asked him to do, but he was unable to. Please remember, *idols cannot walk.* Gunther did not say he was struggling with idols in his life, but I believe he got healed of an idol that was in his bloodline, of which he was unaware. Why? In that same meeting (and I have the videos to prove it), three people came up on stage and testified that during the healing activation, they had to run out of the room to go to the bathroom. When they urinated, it smelled strongly like ammonia!

Idols Mess with Your Spiritual Gifts

Now there are distinctive varieties and distributions of endowments (gifts, extraordinary powers distinguishing certain Christians, due to the power of divine grace operating in their souls by the Holy Spirit) and they vary, but the [Holy] Spirit remains the same.

1 Corinthians 12:4

Once again, remember that the Bible says that *idols cannot see, they cannot hear, they cannot walk, they cannot talk.* I have already shown you how these idols can make you blind, deaf, dumb, and crippled in the natural. Now let me show you how these worthless idols and their evil altars in our soul are also affecting your spiritual gifts. Because some of these idols are blind, they can block you from seeing in the spirit and receiving dreams and visions. Others are deaf and dumb spirits like the ones in the epileptic child in Mark 9. So, as you will see, idols not only cause hearing and speech problems in the natural, but they also block you from hearing the voice of God while hindering you from releasing an accurate prophetic word. Since idols can't walk, they can interfere with your spiritual walk with the Lord by leading you off the path of righteousness into sin.

The proof of all these things is found in the Pauline chapter that teaches on spiritual gifts.

"Now about the spiritual gifts (the special endowments of supernatural energy), brethren, I do not want you to be misinformed. 2 You know that when you were heathen, you were led off after idols that could not speak..."

1 Cor 12:1-2 (AMPC)

For the longest time, I was baffled by Paul's strange introduction to the gifts of the Spirit in this passage. In the first verse of 1 Corinthians 12, Paul begins with his desire for the church to flow in the gifts of the Spirit. However, his introduction takes a strange turn in verse two. Paul tells the believers at Corinth that even though he was about to discuss the special gifts of the Spirit, he had a warning for them: *"I do not want you to be misinformed. You know that when you were a heathen, you were led off after idols."* Then he even adds, *"that could not speak!"* Paul was making it VERY clear that any idols in their bloodline and even in their own life were going to interfere with their ability to move in the gifts of the Spirit! Interestingly enough, he emphasized that these idols could not speak, reaffirming my statement that idols can interfere with a believer's ability to prophesy accurately.

Paul knew something about idols that he wants you to know! *"They will block your gifts!"* We need to heed Paul's warning in the church today! If you're going to demonstrate the wonder-working power of God in this earth, you must divorce yourself from every idol you have been pursuing and then be healed of all idols in your bloodline.

Food Offered to Idols

In most cases, the loudest idols that control us are "food idols." Please don't tell me *food is not an idol. The main rituals that always took place in ancient idol-worshipping ceremonies involved feasting.* Idol

11

worshippers always brought food that they dedicated to and sacrificed to an idol. They believed that eating food that was first dedicated to idols enabled them to become one with the demon god the idol represented. Consequentially, they feasted lavishly on the food sacrificed to idols. Do you know what Paul *says* about this practice in 1 Corinthians 10:7? *"Do not be worshipers of false gods as some of them were, as it is written, The people sat down to eat and drink [the sacrifices offered to the golden calf at Horeb] and rose to sport (to dance and give way to jesting and hilarity)."* Excessive eating and drinking are a form of worship the ancients practiced to honor their gods and become one with them. It's the same today; nothing has changed. The demon gods' behind idols are accustom to having food sacrificed to them in worship. So, to get their fix, idols drive you to overeat, even when you're not hungry! They even drive you to consume junk foods and sugars that will cause you to gain weight, develop diabetes, high blood pressure, and high cholesterol.

In 1 Corinthians 10, Paul gave us a severe warning about feasting at the table of idols!

> *"What do I imply then? That food offered to idols is [intrinsically changed by the fact and amounts to] anything or that an idol itself is a [living] thing? 20 No, I am suggesting that what the pagans sacrifice they offer [in effect] to demons (to evil spiritual powers) and not to God [at all]. I do not want you to fellowship and be partners with diabolical spirits [by eating at their feasts]."*

1 Cor 10:19-20

Paul is stating that overeating is not just bad for you; it also has grave spiritual consequences. You can form a fellowship and partnership with diabolic spirits by eating at their feasts! When we turn food into an idol that we use to comfort us and medicate our pain, we are inviting demons to attack every part of our life, including our physical bodies. Food idols can also open the door for Satan to attack our families, marriage, finances, businesses, ministries, and even churches. **Food is one of the most significant ways' idols riot!**

Are demons driving you to eat? I personally lived through this. "I was possessed by a food idol, and I was constantly feasting even when I wasn't hungry." After I got the breakthrough, my whole life changed. I even lost weight supernaturally. Once you break this demonic cycle, you're going to lose weight too supernaturally. Just like that!

Idols have their hand in so many pies it would be impossible to describe them all. Believe me, idols can even cause plaques to come upon your life! Diseases such as tumors, boils, and hemorrhoids afflicting your body may be due to having these idols in your soul! As proof, I offer the story in 1 Samuel 5. The Philistines had just stolen the ark of the covenant from the Israelites. Foolishly they decided to store the highly prized item in the temple of Ashdod right next to the statue of their god Dagon. Unfortunately, it didn't end very well for the Philistines or their demon god. The following day they found their idol fallen, with his face on the ground before the ark of the Lord. The idol's head and hands were cut off! As for the people of Ashdod, the Bible says;

> "...the hand of the Lord was heavy upon the people of
> Ashdod, and He caused [mice to spring up and there was]
> very deadly destruction and He smote the people with [very
> painful] tumors or boils,. ...9 the hand of the Lord was
> against the city, causing an exceedingly great panic [at the
> deaths from the plague], for He afflicted the people of the

city, both small and great, and tumors or boils broke out on them."

1 Sam 5:6,9

Ashdod was filled with mice, which resulted in a city-wide plague. The people were covered with tumors and boils. Many of them died. As painful as this must have been, there was also an unusual breakout of hemorrhoids among the people. The King James Version of this passage says the Lord smote them with *"emerods."* Emerods is the Hebrew word "těchor," which, according to Strong's means, "to burn; a boil or ulcer (from the inflammation), especially a tumor in the anus or pudenda (the piles)." Ouch! I've seen many tumors, skin issues, and hemorrhoids get healed when people were delivered from idols in their soul. Since it was the Lord that smote the Philistines with these sicknesses, you might ask, "Is He doing the same thing to us because of our idolatry?" Nothing could be further from the truth!

The heavenly Father sent His only begotten Son to die for every sin and disease, so He would never put on us what His Son gave His life for! However, our own sins of idolatry can provide a legal ground for the enemy to cause these types of affliction to manifest in our bodies. As you will see, my friend Dr. Myles teaches that spiritual warfare is the result of two opposing altars standing side by side, which is exactly what happened the day the Philistines dared to place the Holy Ark of God next to an altar dedicated to a demon god. Today you are the ark of God that carries His presence. Spiritual warfare will always ensue when you allow an idol to come into your life. Throughout the rest of this book, Dr. Francis Myles and I will show you how these idols get their legal rights through evil altars planted in your soul and bloodline. These idols also get their legal rights through "accusations" generated by your lawbreaking to control and devastate every area of your life! As you continue to read, we will show you how you can re-position yourself to get healed and delivered of all these idols and evil altars.

Idols steal your spiritual gifts.

Life Application Section

Memory Verse

You shall have no other gods before or besides Me. [4] *You shall not make yourself any graven image [to worship it] or any likeness of anything that is in the heavens above, or that is in the earth beneath, or that is in the water under the earth;* [5] *You shall not bow down yourself to them or serve them; for I the Lord your God am a jealous God, visiting the iniquity of the fathers upon the children to the third and fourth generation of those who hate Me.* Exodus 20:30-5

Reflections

1. What is an idol?

_____

_____

_____

_____

_____

2. Name some things idols can do to control and devastate our lives?

_____

_____

_____

_____

_____

Prayer of Release # 1

Breaking The First Commandment

"Heavenly Father, I ask for the Court of Heaven to be seated and the books to be opened as I come before the Judge of all the earth to plead my case so I can be justified and proven right. I am here in court with my official representative, the Holy Spirit, who is my advocate and my counselor. Heavenly Father, I surrender all rights to self-representation; instead, I ask my defense attorney and mediator of the new covenant, the Lord Jesus Christ, to represent me in your Royal Courtroom. Heavenly Father, I bring my case to your Supreme Court and to your Grace Court to face all charges and prosecute all idols and evil altars that are controlling my life and bloodline, in Jesus' Name. I am seeking deliverance from any soul wounds that have caused me to break Your first commandment. I am seeking a verdict of release from this Court.

I now enter a plea of 'guilty' into the court's records. The Bible says in Matthew 5:25, *"Come to terms quickly* [at the earliest opportunity] *with your opponent at law while you are with him on the way* [to court]*, so that your opponent does not hand you over to the judge, and the judge to the guard, and you are thrown into prison."*

Lord, since I am under oath, I cannot lie about my sinful activities and the iniquities of my bloodline that are connected to idolatry and erecting evil altars. I agree with any legitimate accusations brought by Satan against me and my bloodline. I submit a plea of guilty to all of Satan's charges that are connected to any idolatry that my ancestors or I ever committed. I now formally submit my guilty plea to the court, in

---

17

Jesus name. It is also written: *And they overcame him by the blood of the Lamb and by the word of their testimony, and they did not love their lives to the death.* Revelation 12:11

As I am called to testify in the witness stand, I first humbly repent of all the charges leveled against me so that I can overcome the enemy through the power of the blood and the word of my testimony. I repent for breaking the first commandment and setting up altars in my life and bloodline that are connected with all demon gods that have caused me vision problems both in the natural and in the spirit. I repent for setting up altars in my life and bloodline that are connected with all demon gods that have caused me any kind of deafness in the natural and in the spirit. I repent for worshipping idols and setting up altars in my life and bloodline that are connected with all demon gods that have caused me any kind of speech problems in the natural and in the spirit. I repent for worshipping idols and setting up altars in my life and bloodline that are connected with all demon gods that have caused me to be crippled in the natural and in the spirit. I repent for worshipping idols and setting up altars in my life and bloodline that are connected with all demon gods that have been messing with my natural and spiritual gifts. I repent for worshipping idols and setting up altars in my life and bloodline that are connected with all demon gods that have caused me to eat and be addicted to foods offered to idols both in the natural and in the spirit. Heavenly Father, I place my sin and that of my ancestral bloodline under the blood of Jesus so I can overcome the enemy through my redeemers' blood. In Jesus' Name."

As I continue to testify in this court, I also decree that I am under the power of the free and unmerited Grace of God. Since the Bible says it's impossible to keep the whole law, I need your redemptive grace. I decree that where my sin of idolatry has increased and abounded; Your Grace has increased the more to overshadow my sin and even superabound over it. I also decree Romans 4:16 over myself. It is written:

> *Therefore, [inheriting] the promise is the outcome of faith and depends [entirely] on faith, in order that it might be given as an act of grace (unmerited favor), to make itstable and valid and guaranteed to all his descendants—not only to the devotees and adherents of the Law, but also to those who share the faith of Abraham, who is [thus] the father of us all.*

Heavenly Father, Righteous Judge, I decree that because of the blood of Jesus and the power of His grace, I must be acquitted of all charges of breaking the first commandment and not placing God first in my life. Because of the blood of Jesus Christ and grace, I must be acquitted of the offense of breaking the first commandment, in Jesus name. And I must be acquitted of all charges of idolatry in Jesus' Name."

Now, Invite Jesus To Heal Your Soul!

"Holy Spirit, I now invite you to search my soul (my will, mind, and emotions) and judge every idol and evil altar that causes my soul to break the first commandment. I surrender every soul wound to you, Lord, for its You, who leads me beside the still waters and restores my soul. Lord Jesus, I am asking You to cleanse my soul with your blood, to cleanse my soul of every sin of idolatry, and to cleanse my soul of every evil altar that has been erected in my inner man. The Bible says it's the blood that atones for the soul. The Bible also declares that the blood cleanses my conscience; thus, I decree the blood is cleansing my mind right now of all thoughts connected to idolatry. I decree the blood is cleansing my will so that it won't be controlled by demon gods. I declare the blood is also cleansing my emotions to sever them from the control of idols and evil altars. Lord Jesus, I am asking You to also use Your "Dunamis Power" according to Acts 10:38 to heal every wound in my soul that the devil uses to oppress me. I also decree Ephesians 3:16 over myself that my soul is being strengthened and re-enforced by mighty Dunamis Power through the Holy Spirit. Thus, I am being strengthened in every place that my soul has been wounded through trauma so that the devil cannot use the pain of my trauma to drive me to idolatry. I also decree that mighty Dunamis Power is re-enforcing my soul to resist all temptations of idolatry. Finally, I decree and declare that I am full of the light of Christ and that my will, mind, and emotions are sound and fulfilling their office because my whole body is full of His light. I release the light of Christ into any darkness in my soul that came from idolatry, in Jesus' Name. Amen.

Because my soul is being healed, I decree that I will never again worship idols nor set up evil altars in my life and bloodline that are connected to any demon god that can cause me any kind of deafness in the natural and in the spirit. I decree that I will never again worship idols nor set up evil altars in my life and bloodline that are connected to any demon god that can cause me any kind of speech problems in the natural and in the spirit. I decree that I will never again worship idols nor set up evil altars in my life and bloodline that are connected to any demon god that can cause me to be crippled in the natural and in the spirit. I decree that I will never again worship idols nor set up evil altars in my life and bloodline that are connected to any demon god that can mess with my natural and spiritual gifts. I decree that I will never again worship idols nor set up evil altars in my life and bloodline that are connected to any demon god that can cause me to eat and be addicted to foods offered to idols. I will never again lift my soul to an idol or demon spirit that is connected to an evil altar."

Loudly Declare These Supernatural Decrees So You Can Have Your Breakthrough!

Heavenly Father

- I decree and declare that the power of idolatry is broken over my life and that I am no longer guilty of breaking the first commandment.

- I decree and declare that you are setting me free from idols that cause physical and spiritual deafness in Jesus' Name.

- I decree and declare that you are setting me free from idols that cause physical and spiritual blindness in Jesus' Name.

- I decree and declare that you are setting me free from idols that cause physical and spiritual muteness in Jesus' Name.

- I decree and declare that as I bring my sacrificial offering into the Courts of Heaven, the power of evil altars over my finances is permanently destroyed.

- I decree and declare that you are setting me free from idols that cause me to be physically or spiritually crippled in Jesus' Name.

- I decree and declare that you are setting me free from food idols that cause me to be addicted to food to medicate unhealed soul wounds, in Jesus' Name.

Time to Take Communion

"Lord, as I take this communion, I do it in remembrance of You and Your victory on the cross and the resurrection. I decree that as I drink this cup of Your blood and eat Your body, my sins are forgiven, and my soul is nourished and refreshed and strengthened. I decree that as I eat Your flesh and drink Your blood, I will never be hungry and thirsty for idols again. I decree that as I partake of Your supper that my "Not Guilty" verdict from this Court concerning "Breaking the first commandment" will be sealed by the power and testimony of Your Body and Blood in Jesus' Name."

2

Window Shopping for Idols

By

Dr. Francis Myles

Those who escorted Paul brought him as far as Athens; and receiving instructions for Silas and Timothy that they should come to him as soon as possible, they departed. [16]Now while Paul was awaiting them at Athens, his spirit was grieved and roused to anger as he saw that the city was full of idols.

Acts 17:15-16

HAVE YOU EVER walked through a shopping mall, with no desire to buy anything, only to return home with items charged to your credit card you didn't need? Women frequently encounter this dilemma, often wondering how it happened. However, in actuality, this impulse shopping phenomenon knows no gender. Heaven knows I have been guilty of bringing home items from the grocery store that ended up spoiling or went unused; yet, at the time, the purchase seemed urgent and needful. Aware of this psychological phenomenon, merchandisers create enticing displays to ensure those passing by the store will have a "wow" moment as their eyes feast on things they desire but do not need.

The Apostle Paul experienced a similar phenomenon when he arrived in the city of Athens, Greece. Paul's spirit was stirred deeply because of the multitude of idols that decorated the Grecian marketplace. Even though Paul had been to cities with idols before, the level of idolatry in the intellectual city of Athens was staggering! Coincidentally, it seems that the more intellectual and secular a nation becomes, the more it floods itself with idols. In some cases, people in liberal, secular societies conceal the truth of their idols by calling them art or entertainment; when in actuality, the spirit driving them is idolatry! We live in a society where we can easily shop for idols on TV, social media, the Internet, and even in the world of sports, without ever leaving our home! We will now explore a small list of some of our most famous idols. Our study will prove that times may have changed, but the demon-gods behind all of our popular cultural idols are essentially the same.

Idols of Reason

So he reasoned and argued in the synagogue with the Jews and those who worshiped there, and in the marketplace [where assemblies are held] day after day with any who chanced to be there.

Acts 17:17

One of the idols that Apostle Paul encountered in Athens is *the idol of reason.* The people of Athens loved to reason and to argue endlessly. Daily they were involved in arguing with each other over science, social, and cultural norms. They even debated on spiritual things they didn't fully understand. If hell can testify, it will tell us that it is full of men and women who would have been saved by the grace of the Lord

Jesus Christ except for their human reasoning. *They reasoned themselves out of believing in Jesus.* The city of Athens was full of intellectual elites who loved and worshipped their educational pedigrees. The idol of reason is especially dangerous when it comes to matters of faith because faith requires a person to believe in the invisible evidence of God's Word.

Unfortunately, intellectuals and people addicted to the idol of reason have a difficult time receiving anything by faith. Believing in a God who requires faith to experience Him is frankly insulting to their educated minds. It is no wonder Apostle Paul declares in 1 Corinthians 1:20-21.

> *"Where is the wise man (the philosopher)? Where is the scribe (the scholar)? Where is the investigator (the logician, the debater) of this present time and age? Has not God shown up the nonsense and the folly of this world's wisdom?*[21] *For when the world with all its earthly wisdom failed to perceive and recognize and know God by means of its own philosophy, God in His wisdom was pleased through the foolishness of preaching [salvation, procured by Christ and to be had through Him], to save those who believed (who clung to and trusted in and relied on Him).*

Idols of Philosophy

And some also of the Epicurean and Stoic philosophers encountered him and began to engage in discussion. And some said, "What is this babbler with his scrap-heap learning trying to say? Others said, He seems to be an announcer of

> *foreign deities—because he preached Jesus and the resurrection."*
>
> Acts 17:18

According to dictionary.com, "philosophy" is defined as *the rational investigation of the truths and principles of being, knowledge, or conduct.* There are three branches of philosophy, a) natural, b) moral, and c) metaphysical, that are widely accepted as composing this study. Unfortunately, philosophy fails and gets hijacked by demons at its point of origin if the foundational assumptions behind it are wrong. For instance, Epicureans philosophers Paul found in Greece said the flesh was naturally evil and uncontrollable and therefore allowed no restrictions of any kind to the fulfillment of its fleshly desires. This philosophy led to all sorts of evil, especially unrelenting indulgence in sexual orgies of any kind.

If hell could testify, it would tell us that it is full of people who reasoned themselves out of believing in Jesus!

Soon enough, the Satanic philosophy of the Epicureans contaminated the doctrine of the Church in Corinth and produced Christians who had no self-restraint where indulging their fleshly desires was concerned. This philosophy polluted the church to such an extent that in Corinth, Paul confronted a young man who was having sexual relations with his mother! Even worse, no one in the church at Corinth confronted this so-called Christian brother because the church leaders were raised under the Epicurean philosophical thinking! *It is actually reported that there is sexual immorality among you, impurity of a sort that is condemned and does not occur even among the heathen; for a*

man has [his own] father's wife. ²And you are proud and arrogant! And you ought rather to mourn (bow in sorrow and in shame) until the person who has done this [shameful] thing is removed from your fellowship and your midst! 1 Corinthians 5:1-2

You may think this is only something the ancient church had to deal with, however, during a conversation with Katie Souza, we both shared how much sexual perversion is devastating today's church. Major church leaders whose names you would recognize are being exposed publicly. And their sins go well beyond a single adulterous affair. They have wantonly stepped into sexting, spouse swapping, child abuse, and even built networks around them consisting of other believers they have recruited to participate in their perversions.

Philosophy and the Idols of "isms"

From that time Jesus began to preach, crying out, Repent change your mind for the better, heartily amend your ways, with abhorrence of your past sins), for the kingdom of heaven is at hand.

Matthew 4:17

Philosophy can create an idolatrous culture. For example, Greek philosophers such as Socrates, Cleisthenes, Plato, and Aristotle created idols of reason, metaphysics, intellectualism, and philosophy. While some of these idols had a detrimental effect on the culture, according to Wikipedia, *Cleisthenes was an ancient Athenian lawgiver credited with reforming the constitution of ancient Athens and setting it on a democratic footing in 508 BC. For these accomplishments, historians refer to him as "the father of Athenian democracy."* The impact these men still have on the worldview of people and the criteria upon which they judge their experience continues to lead many to idolize reason, logic, and philosophy over the teachings of Christ. Then we have men like Karl Marx (socialism/communism), Mussolini (fascism), and Hitler (nazism) whose ideology led to the slaughter of millions of people, enslavement of many, and the financial exploitation of the many by the few. My spiritual mentor, the late Dr. Myles Munroe, said, "the world we live in is ruled by dead men!"

On a human level, the philosophy of democracy has resulted in the least flawed forms of human government by allowing the many (electorate) to choose and elect their political representatives through an open and fair electoral process. However, democracy has also produced a very formidable "idol" that competes with God's Sovereignty, making it difficult for God's children to truly submit to the authority of the Holy Spirit. What is the idol I am referencing here? To locate the idol, we first must analyze the two forms of government, democratic versus kingdom government. *Democratic government is essentially the rule of the people by the people.* In a democratic government, the "majority rules!" Unfortunately, this type of government is diametrically opposed to the sovereign government of kingdoms, such as the Kingdom of God! In kingdoms, the government is solely on the shoulders of the king. Isaiah 9:6 *"For to us a Child is born, to us a Son is given; and the government shall be upon His shoulder, and His name shall be called Wonderful Counselor, Mighty God, Everlasting Father [of Eternity], Prince of Peace."*

When a person is raised in a democratic representative government comes to faith in the Messiah-Jesus, the war between their idol "self-determination" and the Kingdom's prerequisite of "total dependency" on God immediately ensues. Christians from democratic societies suddenly find themselves at odds with a God who can care less about what they think! They are shocked to discover that Messiah-Jesus did not save them from sin, so He could sanctify their educated opinions and use them to advance His Kingdom. God wants them to trust and obey, even when doing so makes no present, discernible sense! For many of them, the "idol" of democracy that sits on their heart is quickly offended. I am a naturalized citizen of the United States, and I must state emphatically that I love the U.S.A. However, we must never forget that our entire system of government was formulated out of rebellion against a kingdom (The United Kingdom of Great Britain). Consequently, in the American psyche, there is an inbuilt distrust for anything that looks like a kingdom, thus, making living and surrendering to the principles of God's Kingdom very difficult for Americans and most Westerners!

According to Wikipedia, socialism is a political, social, and economic philosophy encompassing a range of economic and social systems characterized by social ownership of the means of production and workers' self-management of enterprises. It includes the political theories and movements associated with such a system. Social ownership can be public, collective, cooperative, or of equity. While no single definition encapsulates many types of socialism, social ownership is the one common element. Greek philosophers such as Plato and Aristotle are credited with this type of thinking. Unfortunately, in every nation on earth where this "ism" has fully materialized, such as Venezuela or Cuba, it has led to abject poverty, starvation, suppression of individual rights and enterprise, chronic dependence on government social welfare programs, and a very repressive nanny State. This "ism" produces two powerful idols, namely, "government dependence" and "entitlement" among a host of other idols.

According to Wikipedia, communism derives from the French communisme, which developed out of the Latin root "communis" and the suffix "isme." It was used as a term designating various social situations before it came to be associated with more modern conceptions of an economic and political organization. Semantically, communis can be translated to "of or for the community" while isme is a suffix that indicates the abstraction into a state, condition, action, or doctrine, so communism may be interpreted as "the state of being of or for the community.'. This semantic constitution has led to various usages of the word in its evolution, but it ultimately came to be most closely associated with Marxism, most specifically embodied in The Communist Manifesto.

Unfortunately, this "ism" has been catastrophic, much more so than socialism. Ruthless communist regimes have killed millions of people. Communism, without fail, produces ruthless, totalitarian super-states such as the Soviet Union and communist China. Under this "ism" the most famous idol is the "State." Individuals lose their God-given free will to become robotic machines of the super-state! Any deviation from the political dogma of the super-state is squashed violently. Consequently, the first victim of communism is the belief in a God who is supreme and above the super-state. A God such as the God of the Bible who supports the idea of individual freedom and self-determination is the biggest threat to a communist state. Consequentially, the philosophy of "communism" breeds another inevitable "ism" called "atheism." Atheism is the belief that there is no God, and "self" is the face of this godless idol! Millions of Christians and Jews were martyred behind the curtains of the cold-war Soviet Union and China, for simply believing that there is a God who is higher than the State! *The [empty-headed] fool has said in his heart, there is no God".* Psalm 14:1

Idols of Sexual Perversion

And by them the glory and majesty and excellence of the immortal God were exchanged for and represented by images, resembling mortal man and birds and beasts and reptiles. [24]Therefore God gave them up in the lusts of their [own] hearts to sexual impurity, to the dishonoring of their bodies among themselves [abandoning them to the degrading power of sin], [25]Because they exchanged the truth of God for a lie and worshiped and served the creature rather than the Creator, Who is blessed forever! Amen (so be it). [26]For this reason God gave them over and abandoned them to vile affections and degrading passions. For their women exchanged their natural function for an unnatural and abnormal one, [27]And the men also turned from natural relations with women and were set ablaze (burning out, consumed) with lust for one another— men committing shameful acts with men and suffering in their own bodies and personalities the inevitable consequences and penalty of their wrong doing and going astray, which was [their] fitting retribution. [28]And so, since they did not see fit to acknowledge God or approve of Him or consider Him worth the knowing, God gave them over to a base and condemned mind to do things not proper or decent but loathsome,

Romans 1:23-28

One of the most potent "idols" that seems to rule every generation of men is the idol of "sexual perversion." Have you noticed that many TV commercials "sexualize" their products while advertising them for public consumption? A car is being advertised on TV when suddenly a scantily dressed woman shows up next to the vehicle: the message is loud and clear. Buying the car is like having sex with a beautiful woman. If these commercials were not effective in generating sales, advertisers would have suspended this strategy a long-time ago.

We live in such a sexualized culture that being homosexual or lesbian or transgender is now mainstream. However, in Romans 1:22-28, the Apostle Paul is very clear, by the Holy Spirit, that the same-sex lifestyle is rooted in idolatry, which is rooted in worshipping alternative sexual preferences against the prescribed biblical standard that sex is between male and female. Even though sex between males and females can also be sinful when it is practiced outside of the covenant of marriage, it is, however, a biblical norm. Please take note of how Apostle Paul in Romans 1:23-24 connects "worshipping idols" to sexual impurity, such as same-sex relations. *"And by them the glory and majesty and excellence of the immortal God were exchanged for and represented by images, resembling mortal man and birds and beasts and reptiles. Therefore God gave them up in the lusts of their [own] hearts to sexual impurity, to the dishonoring of their bodies among themselves."*

Based on the current social norms, some will accuse me of homophobia. I am not! I love every human being created by God regardless of their sexual orientation. As a United States citizen, I sincerely respect the civil rights of every American. Nevertheless, as a citizen of the Kingdom of God, I must also point out what scripture says about our social norms from a Kingdom perspective! Sadly, I am not surprised that in countries like Canada, pastors can go to jail for quoting Romans 1:22-28 in a sermon. They will be accused of spewing hate! Thankfully, pedophilia (*the sexual exploitation of children*) is still illegal in most law-abiding nations. But mark my words, the demon of sexual perversion is a master at the art of pushing the envelope of sexual norms. Even now, there is a move to make "pedophilia" a legally protected sexual orientation.

Sadly, the idol of sexual perversion has also infected the Body of Christ worldwide. When the Holy Spirit pulls back the curtains of

One of the most potent idols that seem to rule every generation of men is the idol of sexual perversion.

sexual perversion, you will be shocked and sick to your stomach when you discover rampant sexual immorality among the clergy. Katie Souza and I became aware of very well-known Charismatic preachers (men of the cloth) who are engaged in habitual wife-swapping and sexual orgies with some of their church members! If we named names, many of you reading this book would scream, oh no! Many of these preachers are using the so-called grace-message to justify these illicit sexual affairs. It seems to me that the demons of the Epicurean Christians are sweeping through Pentecostal and Charismatic circles. This is one of the many reasons why Katie and I felt led of the LORD to write this book, "Idols Riot!"

Institutional Idols

And they took hold of him and brought him to the Areopagus [Mars Hill meeting place], saying, may we know what this novel (unheard of and unprecedented) teaching is which you are openly declaring?

Acts 17:19

According to Wikipedia, In 2019, a scandal arose over a criminal conspiracy to influence undergraduate admissions decisions at several top American universities. The investigation into the conspiracy was nicknamed Operation Varsity Blues. The investigation and related charges were made public on March 12, 2019, by United States federal prosecutors. At least 53 people have been charged as part of the conspiracy, many of whom pleaded guilty or agreed to plead guilty. Thirty-three parents of college applicants are accused of paying more than $25 million between 2011 and 2018 to William Rick Singer, organizer of the scheme. He used part of the money to fraudulently inflate entrance exam test scores and bribe college officials. What would make famous movie stars, such as Felicity Hoffman and business leaders, risk criminal prosecution to commit bribery so their children could get into an Ivy League university? The answer is obvious: these Ivy league universities represent "institutional idols" that are worshipped by the intellectual and social elite of our modern times.

You can clearly discern this "institutional idolatry" in the disdainful look that graduates from Harvard and Yale direct towards graduates from so-called lesser universities. There are social circles of influence in America that are entirely closed to persons who did not graduate from famous Ivy League universities. It's no wonder these desperate parents were willing to cheat and bribe their way into securing college admission for their children in the chambers of these "institutional idols." There are students and parents in America who are living under very strenuous financial debt due to attending school at these "institutional idols." Their idolization of these Ivy League universities has robbed them of freedom and sentenced them to a life of debt. Paul faced this same "institutional idol" in the city of Athens, when he was brought before Greek intellectual elites at a famous institution of learning known as the Areopagus [Mars Hill meeting place]. The Mars Hill was the birthplace of Greek philosophies that still influence much of today's secular thinking!

Idols that Tickle the Ear!

For you set forth some startling things, foreign and strange to our ears; we wish to know therefore just what these things mean. ²¹For the Athenians, all of them, and the foreign residents and visitors among them spent all their leisure time in nothing except telling or hearing something newer than the last.

Acts 17:20-21

One of the idols that Paul faced in Athens was the idol that the Bible says will be very common in the last days before the second coming of Messiah-Jesus! It's the idol the Bible calls the "spirit of the itching ear!" This is an idol that conditions men's spirits and souls to listen only to what "tickles" their ears without bringing them into the knowledge of the truth. This idol causes people to be "ever-learning but never coming to the knowledge of the truth." In 2 Timothy 4:3-4, the Bible declares, *"For the time is coming when [people] will not tolerate (endure) sound and wholesome instruction, but, having ears itching [for something pleasing and gratifying], they will gather to themselves one teacher after another to a considerable number, chosen to satisfy their own liking and to foster the errors they hold, And will turn aside from hearing the truth and wander off into myths and man-made fictions."*

This idol of the itching ear that Paul confronted in Athens is evident today as the Body of Messiah-Jesus is full of church hoppers, those who can never submit to godly authority. Instead, they church-hop until they find a church governed by a pastor who will tell them whatever they want to hear. This idol makes it difficult for people to digest the truth of the gospel of Jesus Christ.

COVID-19 Exposes Our Idols

Without a doubt, there has never been a virus in my lifetime that has rapidly changed the world, killed thousands, and shaken the economies of nations, like the Coronavirus, widely referred to as COVID-19. While trying to stem the tide of this killer virus, governments went into panic mode. They all began to issue national lockdowns and stay-at-home population quarantines. Since one of the keys to containing the spread of the virus is "social distancing," governments banned big public gatherings. These social distancing bans shut down most businesses, including sports and entertainment activities. Church gatherings were also temporarily banned. In so doing, the virus exposed our cultural addictions to the idols of sports, arts, and entertainment. Since the stay-home quarantines, alcohol consumption in the United States, according to Statista, increased by over 75%[i] because many people were depressed because the social outlets they use to comfort their souls were shut down due to the outbreak. Suicides also rose exponentially[ii]!

Worshipping Demons

So Paul, standing in the center of the Areopagus [Mars Hill meeting place], said: Men of Athens, I perceive in every way [on every hand and with every turn I make] that you are most religious or very reverent to demons.

Acts 17:22

When Paul began to challenge the idolatrous structures of the ancient city of Athens, he unraveled the mystery behind their idolatrous passions- *they were unknowingly worshipping demons*. Suddenly, their city of idols was no longer an issue of different tastes in art or philosophy. Paul wanted them to know that they were actually worshipping demonic entities with malicious intent towards the human race. Consequentially, all idol worship is either directly or indirectly related to a demonic entity that serves as the power source behind the thing we idolize. It's no wonder God hates idolatry because idols steal the glory that rightfully belongs to Him while causing men to fellowship with demons. The Holy Spirit wants to set us free from all our idols, which are afflicting us with passions and mindless thoughts that we cannot control. Let's face it, *"idols are literary driving us crazy!"*

Jesus Among Other gods!

For as I passed along and carefully observed your objects of worship, I came also upon an altar with this inscription, To the unknown god. Now what you are already worshiping as unknown, this I set forth to you. [24]*The God Who produced and formed the world and all things in it, being Lord of heaven and earth, does not dwell in handmade shrines. 25Neither is He served by human hands, as though He lacked anything, for it is He Himself Who gives life and breath and all things to all [people].*

Acts 17:23-24

The above scripture makes it clear why God wants every member of the Body of Messiah-Jesus to confront the idols in our soul and culture. By their own admission, the Grecians thought "Jesus" whom Paul preached was just another idol in desperate need of recognition and cultural relevance. Nothing could have been further from the truth! Jesus is not an idol. He is God incarnate, creator of the universe, and everything in it! These unsaved Greek intellectuals were headed towards hellfire and a Godless eternity if they did not receive Messiah-Jesus as their personal Lord and Savior. But how could they accept Jesus, when He was surrounded by so many other competing deities? Doesn't this describe the current spiritual condition of the world we live in today? It's time to tear down the altars of these competing idols, so the glorious light of Jesus can shine in our souls like a city set on a hill!

Life Application Section

Memory Verses

Now while Paul was awaiting them at Athens, his spirit was grieved and roused to anger as he saw that the city was full of idols. Acts 17:16

He also is the Head of [His] body, the church; seeing He is the Beginning, the Firstborn from among the dead, so that He alone in everything and in every respect might occupy the chief place [stand first and be preeminent]. Colossians 1:18

Reflections

1. Are there any idols in your life competing with Jesus?

_____

_____

_____

_____

_____

2. Name three idols that Paul confronted in Athens.

_____

_____

_____

_____

Prayer of Release # 2

Window Shopping for Idols

"Heavenly Father, I ask for the Court of Heaven to be seated and the books to be opened as I come before the Judge of all the earth to plead my case so I can be justified and proven right. I am here in court with my official representative, the Holy Spirit, who is my advocate and counselor. Heavenly Father, I surrender all rights to self-representation; instead, I ask my defense attorney and mediator of the new covenant, the Lord Jesus Christ, to represent me in your Royal Courtroom. Heavenly Father, I bring my case to your Supreme Court and to your Grace Court to face all charges and prosecute all idols and evil altars that are controlling my life and bloodline, in Jesus' Name. I am seeking deliverance from any soul wounds that have caused me to window shop for idols. I am seeking a verdict of release from this Court.

I now enter a plea of 'guilty' into the court's records. The Bible says in Matthew 5:25, *"Come to terms quickly* [at the earliest opportunity] *with your opponent at law while you are with him on the way* [to court]*, so that your opponent does not hand you over to the judge, and the judge to the guard, and you are thrown into prison."*

Lord, since I am under oath, I cannot lie about my sinful activities and the iniquities of my bloodline that are connected to idolatry and erecting evil altars. I agree with any legitimate accusations brought by Satan against me and my bloodline. I submit a plea of guilty to all of Satan's charges that are connected to any idolatry that my ancestors or I ever committed. I now formally submit my guilty plea to the court, in Jesus name." It is also written: *And they overcame him by the blood of the Lamb and by the word of their testimony, and they did not love their lives to the death.* Revelation 12:11

As I am called to testify on the witness stand, I first humbly repent of all the charges leveled against me so that I can overcome the enemy through the power of the blood and the word of my testimony. I repent of all personal and generational sin connected to window shopping for idols. I repent for violating the order of first things and for not giving God first place in my life. I repent for flirting with idolatry. I repent for lusting after idols of reason, institutional idols of sports and entertainment, idols of philosophy, institutional idols of education, and idols of isms, such as Marxism, Communism, Socialism, and Atheism. I repent for idols that tickle the ears and for allowing Satan to put itching ears in my soul that have addicted me to the doctrine of demons while rejecting the truth of God's word. I also repent for all food idols that are destroying the temple of my body. I repent for every time I have defiled my temple with idols of sexual perversion and allowing myself to be controlled by the demons behind those perversions. Heavenly Father, I place my sin and that of my ancestral bloodline under the blood of Jesus so I can overcome the enemy through my Redeemers' blood. In Jesus' Name.

As I continue to testify in this court, I also decree that I am under the power of the free and unmerited Grace of God. Since the Bible says it's impossible to keep the whole law, I need your redemptive grace. I decree that where my sin of idolatry has increased and abounded, Your Grace has increased the more to overshadow my sin and even superabound over it. I also decree Romans 3:20 and 24 over myself. It is written: *For no person will be justified (made righteous, acquitted, and judged acceptable) in His sight by observing the works prescribed by the*

Law. [24] *[All] are justified and made upright and in right standing with God, freely and gratuitously by His grace (His unmerited favor and mercy), through the redemption which is [provided] in Christ Jesus,*

Heavenly Father, Righteous Judge, I decree that because of the blood of Jesus and the power of His grace, I must be acquitted of all charges of window shopping for idols and not placing God first in my life. Because of the blood of Jesus Christ and His grace, I must be acquitted of the offense of violating the order of first things in Jesus' Name. And I must be acquitted of all charges of idolatry in Jesus' Name.

Now, Invite Jesus To Heal Your Soul!

Holy Spirit, I now invite you to search my soul (my will, mind, and emotions) and judge every idol and evil altar that causes my soul to window shop for idols. I surrender every soul wound to you, Lord, for it is You who leads me beside the still waters and restores my soul. Lord Jesus, I am asking You to cleanse my soul with Your blood, to cleanse my soul of every sin of idolatry, and to cleanse my soul of every evil altar that has been erected in my inner man. The Bible says it's the blood that atones for the soul. The Bible also declares that the blood cleanses my conscience; thus, I decree the blood is cleansing my mind right now of all thoughts connected to idolatry. I decree the blood is cleansing my will so that demon gods won't control it. I declare the blood is also cleansing my emotions to sever them from the control of idols and evil altars. Lord Jesus, I am asking You to also use Your "Dunamis Power," according to Acts 10:38, to heal every wound in my soul that the devil uses to oppress me. I also decree Ephesians 3:16 over myself that my soul is being strengthened and re-enforced by mighty Dunamis Power through the Holy Spirit. Thus, I am being strengthened in every place that my soul has been wounded through trauma so that the devil cannot use the pain of my trauma to drive me to idolatry. I also decree that mighty Dunamis Power is re-enforcing my soul to resist all temptations of idolatry. Finally, I decree and declare that I am full of the light of Christ and that my will, mind, and emotions are sound and fulfilling their office because my whole body is full of His light. I release the light of Christ into any darkness in my soul that came from idolatry, in Jesus' Name. Amen

Right now, because my soul is being healed, I decree that I will not lust after idols of reason. I declare that I am healed of institutional idols of sports, entertainment, and education. I declare that I am healed of idols of sexual perversion. I declare that I am healed of idols of philosophy, as well as idols of isms, such as Marxism, Communism, Socialism, and Atheism. I declare that I am healed from idols that tickle the ears, and from all food idols that are destroying the temple of my body, in Jesus' Name, I pray."

Loudly Declare These Supernatural Decrees So You Can Have Your Breakthrough!

Heavenly Father…

- I decree and declare that the influence of food idols is broken over my life, and therefore I will lose weight supernaturally, I have control over my food intake. I despise junk food, fast food, and sugar. I only desire healthy and nutritious food.

- I decree and declare that the influence of institutional idols of education is broken over my life, so my education is blessed, and I have admission to the schools that God wrote in my book of destiny. All my educational expenses are paid in full.

- I decree and declare that the influence of idols of sexual perversion is broken over my life, so I no longer lust for the things considered unholy by God. I walk in purity and uprightness before the Lord and all mankind.

- I decree and declare that the influence of idols of philosophy is broken over my life, so I will no longer bring my democratic thinking into the Kingdom. I will no longer be ruled by the demonic philosophies of this world that are contrary to Christ.

- I decree and declare that the influence of idols of reason is broken over my life and that I am no longer a prisoner of my logic. I can quickly recognize the voice of the Holy Spirit and follow His leading.

- I decree and declare that all idols of Communism, Marxism, Socialism are broken over my life. I no longer look to the government or other people to take care of my needs.

- I decree and declare that the influence of sports and TV idols are broken over my life. I enjoy partaking in the things of God: worship, Bible study, and even going to church. I also enjoy watching clean entertainment and engaging in any activity that is pure but also fun.

- I decree and declare that since I am free of the drive to window shop for idols, I can now totally focus on God and living in the Secret Place.

Time to Take Communion

"Lord, as I take this communion, I do it in remembrance of you and your victory on the cross and the resurrection. I decree that as I drink this cup of your blood and eat your body, my sins are forgiven, and my soul is nourished and refreshed and strengthened. I decree that as I eat your flesh and drink your blood, I will <u>never be hungry and thirsty for idols again.</u> I decree that as I partake of your supper that my Not Guilty Verdict from this Court concerning "window shopping for idols" will be sealed by the Power and Testimony of Your Body and Blood in Jesus' Name."

THE IDOLS ARE RIOTING

3

The Law of Dominion

by

Dr. Francis Myles

Then God said, "Let Us make man in Our image, according to Our likeness; let them have dominion over the fish of the sea, over the birds of the air, and over the cattle, over all the earth and over every creeping thing that creeps on the earth." So God created man in His own image; in the image of God He created him; male and female He created them. Then God blessed them, and God said to them, "Be fruitful and multiply; fill the earth and subdue it; have dominion over the fish of the sea, over the birds of the air, and over every living thing that moves on the earth."

Genesis 1:26-28 (NKJV)

ๆจๆจๆจ

MY SPIRITUAL MENTOR, the late Dr. Myles Munroe, used to say, "wherever purpose is not known, abuse is inevitable." The genesis of God's purpose for creating the human race can be found in the first two chapters of Genesis. The Genesis account underscores God's inherent motivation to create a physical planet called Earth and create spirit-children that He collectively called "Adam." God then created physical bodies made of dirt to house these spirit-beings so that they could become legal residents and guardians of the visible world. From the beginning, our physical world (earth) was designed to be a spiritual colony of the Kingdom of Heaven. It was never intended to be a habitation of demons and every foul spirit.

Our Dominion Mandate

So God created man in His own image; in the image of God He created him; male and female He created them. Then God blessed them, and God said to them, "Be fruitful and multiply; fill the earth and subdue it; have dominion over the fish of the sea, over the birds of the air, and over every living thing that moves on the earth"

Genesis 1:27-28 (NKJV)

On the sixth day of creation, God created His master species, mankind! In Genesis 1:26-28, we are told that humankind was created by God to be an ambassadorial representative of God's invisible Kingdom on this visible planet, we call Earth. Said simply, we were created to rule over the world of matter on behalf of the Kingdom of God. Created in both the image (God's spiritual essence) and likeness (God's DNA) of God, there were no other creatures that can compete with man's unique position as the son of God. However, it's the gift of dominion that God gave to mankind that I am most interested in pursuing. God said, **"let them have dominion,"** which comes from the Hebrew word "mamlakah," which means ruler, rulership, or kingdom.

The term mamlakah also signifies the area and the people that constitute a "kingdom." It is important to note that the concept of "king" was also considered the embodiment of kingdom. The king was viewed as the "symbol" of the kingdom proper and personified the glory of the kingdom. Therefore, the definition of dominion can be crafted in the following manner:

"To be given dominion means to be established as a sovereign, kingly ruler, master, governor, responsible for reigning over a designated territory, with the inherent authority to represent and embody as a symbol, the territory, resources and all that constitutes that kingdom." (Dr. Myles Munroe, Rediscovering the Kingdom, page 45)

According to God, this dominion mandate upon mankind would rest on four pillars:

1. Being fruitful
8. Multiplying
9. Filling or Replenishing the Earth
10. Subduing the Earth

The Implications of Our Dominion Mandate

Then God said, "Let Us make man in Our image, according to Our likeness; let them have dominion over the fish of the sea, over the birds of the air, and over the cattle, over all the earth and over every creeping thing that creeps on the earth.

Genesis 1:26

The million-dollar question I want you to ask yourself is, "What is the spiritual connection between idols, evil altars, and man's dominion mandate?" When God created Adam and Eve (the first humans) and gave them dominion over this planet, He made an irreversible decree that would impact Him and every celestial (spirit) being in a significant manner. When God transferred dominion (rulership) of this planet to mankind, *He deliberately excluded Himself and every celestial (angelic) being from the Earth's legal authority structure.* God said, **"let them"** have dominion. Please take note of the words *"let them."* This expression excludes God, angels, or spirit beings from interfering in earthly affairs without the legal permission of a man. By using the expression "let them," God locked Himself out of influencing this world without Man's permission. Why would God do such a thing? For two main reasons:

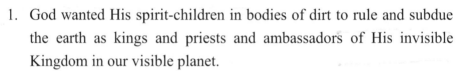

1. God wanted His spirit-children in bodies of dirt to rule and subdue the earth as kings and priests and ambassadors of His invisible Kingdom in our visible planet.

2. God, in His eternal love for us, knew at the time of Adam's creation that Lucifer and one-third of His angels had already fallen from grace and were cast out of heaven. Being a loving Father, God did not want these fallen and malicious spirits to rule the planet He created for mankind. So, He locked them out but never threw away the keys. He simply placed the keys to "loose" (allow legal entry) or "bind" (deny access) in our hands. So, humans are 100% responsible for everything that happens in the world of men – nothing takes place without our permission!

God, Idols, and Altars

For as I passed along and carefully observed your objects of worship, I came also upon an altar with this inscription, To the unknown god. Now what you are already worshiping as unknown, thisI set forth to you. [24]*The God Who produced and formed the world and all things in it, being Lord of heaven and earth, does not dwell in handmade shrines.* [25] *Neither is He served by human hands, as though He lacked anything, for it is He Himself Who gives life and breath and all things to all [people].*

Acts 17:23-24

Since God had just effectively and irrevocably locked Himself and all celestial beings out of the Earth's legal authority structure, how was He to get involved in the affairs of men? Like any good and loving parent, God did not create us and then shrug His shoulders and say, "you are on your own, I am leaving!" God created us first and foremost for intimacy and then to dominate this planet on His behalf so the earth could become a colony of the Kingdom of Heaven. However, by the "Law of Dominion," God could only accomplish both by securing man's permission or cooperation.

The **Law of Dominion** simply means that **spirits without physical bodies of dirt are illegal on earth unless they are functioning through a human.** This is an unbreakable law of God's Kingdom. Suddenly, "prayer" becomes critically essential! It becomes man's way of giving God the legal permission He needs to righteously interfere in the affairs of men. The Law of Dominion effectively transformed the "Earth" into a world or planet of men. *That is why Jesus had to become a man to rescue us legally from the law of sin and death.*

As a result of the far-reaching implications of the *Law of Dominion*, God, in His eternal genius, devised a way for Himself and the holy angels to legally enter our physical planet. *God showed Adam how to build an altar when He killed an animal in the garden of Eden to atone*

51

for their sin. How else did the children of Adam, Cain, and Abel know how to build an altar (Genesis 4)? *The altar, like an airport, would serve as a meeting place between divinity and humanity. It would be a consecrated place where spirits could legally land at man's beckoning.* Since the first altar in the garden of Eden was covered in the blood of atonement, the altar would essentially become a place of death, sacrifice, and redemption.

Since mankind is the legal guardian of this planet, the most important element at any altar is the **human who attends to the altar**.

Spirits without physical bodies of dirt are illegal on Earth unless they are functioning through a human.

The person who serves as the attendant to the altar becomes a priest unto God or the servant of the demonic entity, which has been given legal authority to operate freely in the world of men through the altar. Since there is only One God, any other entity from the kingdom of darkness that is given legal authority through an altar to operate in the world of men, becomes the "idol" (god) behind that altar. Since all altars are essentially power stations, the altar's attendant is supernaturally empowered by either God or the demon-god behind the altar. Until an altar is demolished, God or the demon-gods behind the altar will continue to operate freely in the world of men. **This is the spiritual connection between God, idols, and altars!**

This chapter will give you a prophetic commentary on the subject of godly and evil altars. For an in-depth study on the subject of altars, please get my book entitled, The Battle of Altars: Spiritual Technology for Divine Encounters! Most importantly, I want to use this chapter to demonstrate that you cannot overthrow the power of idols in your life if you fail to address the evil altars in your generational bloodline or the unhealed areas of our soul!

Defining an Altar

And Noah built an altar to the Lord and took of every clean [four-footed] animal and of every clean fowl or bird and offered burnt offerings on the altar. [21] *When the Lord smelled the pleasing odor [a scent of satisfaction to His heart], the Lord said to Himself, I will never again curse the ground because of man, for the imagination (the strong desire) of man's heart is evil and wicked from his youth; neither will I ever again smite and destroy every living thing, as I have done.*

Genesis 8:20-21

Let us first begin by defining the word altar. It is difficult to understand something that we cannot define. So here we go!

An altar is a supernatural landing strip, a power station, a consecrated place, a place of exchange, where spirits (God, angels, or demons) land; it is where humanity meets with divinity!

If you examine any altar, godly or ungodly, it will meet these basic qualifications. It is also easy to identify the kind of altars functioning in your life by the type of spirits, or God encounters, that you keep experiencing.

Godly and Evil Altars

And in the course of time Cain brought to the Lord an offering of the fruit of the ground. [4] *And Abel brought of the firstborn of his flock and of the fat portions. And the Lord had respect and regard for Abel and for his offering,* [5] *But for [Cain and his offering He had no respect or regard. So Cain was exceedingly angry and indignant, and he looked sad and depressed.*

Genesis 4:3-5

In scripture, there are two basic types of altars, righteous and evil altars. The first time in scripture that we are confronted with this distinction is in the fourth chapter of the book of Genesis. This was when the two sons of Adam, Cain, and Abel decided to build altars to offer their sacrificial offerings to the Lord. According to scripture, Cain brought the Lord an offering of the fruit of the ground. Cain, who was an agricultural farmer, placed vegetables on his altar. On the other hand, Abel brought of the firstborn of his flock and of its fatty portions. God's reaction to the offerings placed on the two altars is pretty telling.

God demonstrably rejected Cain's offering, while He accepted and showered Abel's sacrificial offering with the favor of His presence. Why did God reject Cain's offering? God had already cursed the ground in Genesis 3:17. The same ground from which Cain brought his offering. *"And to Adam He said, Because you have listened and given heed to the voice of your wife and have eaten of the tree of which I commanded you, saying, You shall not eat of it, the ground is under a curse because of you; in sorrow and toil shall you eat [of the fruits] of it all the days of your life.*" I am certain, Adam and Eve had already told their sons that the Lord had cursed the ground because of their sin. Why would Cain attempt to atone for his sins by bringing an offering from something already cursed?

The answer: - He was driven by rebellion, pride, and the desire to do his own thing. God's rejection of Cain's offering shows us that He is very selective of what's given to Him at a righteous altar. This act separates God from idols (demon-gods) who will accept any "accursed thing" offered to them by their human attendants. Idols are so desperate for expression in the world of men that they will accept any offering, provided it gains them access to the world of men. On the other hand, God is sovereign, holy, and separate from sinners, so He cannot be manipulated by His human attendants to His altar. He accepted Abel's offering because Abel gave Him what He required for the remission of sins - the blood of an innocent animal, from the best of his flock! Consequentially, Cain became the biblical symbol for an evil and defiled altar. An evil altar is built on wickedness, pride, defiance, rebellion, rage, jealousy, selfish ambition, and murder. The god behind Cain's evil altar was the "idol of self," and ultimately, Satan was Cain's god. Now it becomes clear why Cain resisted and argued with God in a desperate show of Satanic defiance!

An altar is a supernatural
landing strip, a place
where divinity meets
humanity.

The 12 Laws of An Altar

1. All Altars have a dedicated human attendant.

And behold, there came a man of God out of Judah by the word of the Lord to Bethel. Jeroboam stood by the altar to burn incense. [2] The man cried against the altar by the word of the Lord, O altar, altar, thus says the Lord: Behold, a son shall be born to the house of David, Josiah by name; and on you shall he offer the priests of the high places who burn incense on you, and men's bones shall be burned on you.

1 Kings 13:1-2

As a consequence of the law of dominion, all altars require a human attendant. By definition, a human is a spirit being housed in a physical body of dirt. When people die, they lose their humanity (physicalness) and become spirit-beings like angels. When this happens, these former humans become illegal on Earth. So they either graduate to their heavenly home if they accepted Messiah-Jesus when they were alive or are dragged to hell by the idols (demon-gods) they worshipped while they were on Earth. That explains why "Idols (demons) Riot" when they lose control of a human being. They have no one to attend and sacrifice to them at an evil altar; thus, they can't enter the earth or have influence over it!

2. All altars have a guiding or supervising spirit.

That night the Lord said to Gideon, "Take your father's bull, the second bull seven years old, and pull down the altar of Baal that your father has and cut down the Asherah [symbol of the goddess Asherah] that is beside it;" Judges 6:25

No altar is without a guiding or supervising spirit that oversees it. Another reason why God forbids His people from having idols is when we allow idols to build altars in our soul, these demon-gods become the guiding spirits in our life. That is why they are times when Christians struggle with sinful passions that have nothing to do with the character of Christ. Suddenly, you want to smoke a cigarette, or you just want to get drunk. For some, the desire to sleep with a person who is not their spouse suddenly becomes almost overbearing. Who is guiding the soul into wanting these things? Answer: It is the idols and the evil altars that have been built for them in their souls. My friend Katie Souza calls these illicit desires and impulses "idols rioting!"

3. **All altars are powered by the sacrifice(s) of the human attendant(s) who attend to the altar.**

But King David said to Araunah, No, but I will buy it of you for a price. I will not offer burnt offerings to the Lord my God of that which costs me nothing. So David bought the threshing floor and the oxen for fifty shekels of silver. [25] David built there an altar to the Lord and offered burnt offerings and peace offerings. So, the Lord heeded the prayers for the land, and Israel's plague was stayed.

2 Samuel 24:24-25

Without fail, all altars are places of sacrifice. God, or the demonic gods behind the altar, always demands that the human attendant demonstrates their commitment and loyalty to the deity behind the altar. That is why all biblical godly altars were covered with the blood of animals slaughtered in sacrifice to the God of Israel. The altar of the Lord also demanded other types of offerings, such as peace offerings, first-fruits, tithes, alms, and so forth. Since the devil is a master copycat, his evil altars also demand sacrifices and offerings from their human attendants who have granted legal rights to these demon-gods to build altars in their soul or bloodline. Katie and I have dedicated a chapter to show you how idols rob you of your God-given finances or resources.

4. **All attendants to an altar are fed by or provided for by the altar they serve.**

Do you not know that those men who are employed in the services of the temple get their food from the temple? And that those who tend the altar share with the altar [in the offerings brought]?

1 Corinthians 9:13

There is another important aspect that governs all altars. All attendants to an altar are fed by, or provided for by, God or the demon-god over the altar they serve. In the sixth chapter of Matthew's Gospel, Jesus admonished his disciples not to worry about what they were going to eat or wear. Why? He knew this principle of altars; the God or demon-god of that altar feeds and provides for the altar's attendant. Most importantly, the menu at any altar is determined by God or the idol (demon-god) behind the altar.

An attendant to the LORD's altar feeds on righteousness, peace, joy, love, godly prosperity, long-suffering, and so forth. An attendant to an idol's evil altar also eats what the demon-god eats. So, if the idol is a demon of sexual perversion, the attendant will feast on pornography, fornication, adultery, masturbation, even pedophilia in certain instances. Why? Because according to the law of altars, God, or the idol behind the altar, determines the menu. One of the quickest ways to determine whether a person is serving God or an idol is to note what they are addicted to; what foods (appetites) can you not walk away from even to obey Jesus?

5. All altars are places of ritual (perpetual or repetitive activity).

Do not be carried about by different and varied and alien teachings; for it is good for the heart to be established and ennobled and strengthened by means of grace (God's favor and spiritual blessing) and not [to be devoted to] foods [rules of diet and ritualistic meals], which bring no [spiritual] benefit or profit to those who observe them. [10] *We have an altar from which those who serve and worship in the tabernacle have no right to eat.*

Hebrews 13:9-10

We serve a God who is a master of setting the correct background for the revelation He wants you to understand. I was born in Africa, where we were confronted with the realities of evil altars long before we came to Christ. Consequently, I do not have some of the theological hang-ups some Christians in the West seem to have when it comes to the subject of altars. I know that the subject of altars cannot be relegated to the Old Testament and thrown into the dust bins of history. Altars are critical components to connecting Earth to the deity you serve.

One of the things I noticed growing up in Africa is that all altars are places of "ritual." According to dictionary.com, the word "ritual" is defined as "an established or prescribed procedure for religious or other rites." The ritual behind any altar can be quickly discerned by examining the repetitive cycles in people's lives. For instance, King David was an avid worshipper of God, so what was the repetitive ritual in his life? He tells us in Psalms 34:1, *"Lord! I'm bursting with joy over what you've done for me! My lips are full of perpetual praise."*

So how can you use this aspect of altars to discern the number of idols operating in your soul or bloodline? Take inventory of repetitive cycles of behavior or happenings that violate and compete with Messiah-Jesus in your life. For instance, do you find that for one reason or the other, you are constantly blowing up in anger? Do you know what you are? You are an attendant to an idol and altar of anger or rage. Until you allow the Holy Spirit to divorce you from the idol and destroy its altar in your soul, you won't be able to control yourself.

6. All altars speak, whether they are stationary or mobile.

A devout man who venerated God and treated Him with reverential obedience, as did all his household; and he gave much alms to the people and prayed continually to God. [3] About the ninth hour (about 3:00 p.m.) of the day he saw clearly in a vision an angel of God entering and saying to him, Cornelius! [4] And he, gazing intently at him, became frightened and said, "What is it, Lord?" And the angel said to him, "Your prayers and your [generous] gifts to the poor have come up [as a sacrifice] to God and have been remembered by Him.

Acts 10:2-4

All altars speak, whether they are stationary or mobile. What do I mean by this? Since all altars are power stations, places of exchange, and landing strips for God, holy angels, or demon-gods, altars can speak on behalf of the human attendant. In the case of Cornelius, the Roman centurion who built an altar of devotion to God by continually giving alms to the poor and praying daily, the altar in his life began to speak in his favor in the Courts of Heaven. Suddenly, an angel from God showed up in his house. The angel told him that his alms and praying had come before God as a memorial. The angel of the Lord proceeded to tell him to get Peter, who was in Joppa, a neighboring town. When Peter arrived, the Holy Ghost fell upon Cornelius and his entire family. They were all gloriously saved and filled with the Holy Spirit. The altar of the Lord in his life spoke and brought him and his family into the Kingdom of God.

However, the voice of the altars of demons (idols) has a malicious agenda that lines up with Satan's character, which is to kill, steal, and destroy (John 10:10). *So how do you recognize the voice of the idol or evil altar in your soul?* Get into a quiet place and purpose to spend intimate time with the Lord. It won't be long before you begin to hear voices in your heart and mind, telling you about things you forgot to do or should be doing. Thoughts such as these will appear in your mind. "I wonder if there are any notifications or messages for me on Facebook. Do we have tomatoes or onions in the fridge? I wonder if the new Avengers movie is out? Why am I having such strong sexual thoughts or desires for this person when I'm trying to spend time with the Lord? I need to go to Ross or Dillard's and do some shopping before the 50% off sale ends."

Have you ever asked yourself the question, "Why is it so difficult for me to concentrate during my quiet time with the Lord? Most importantly, what is the source of all these distractions?" It's the voices of the idols in your life projected on the screen of your mind from the evil altars in your soul or bloodline!

7. All altars are places of exchange.

And Noah built an altar to the Lord and took of every clean [four-footed] animal and of every clean fowl or bird and offered burnt offerings on the altar. [21] When the Lord smelled the pleasing odor [a scent of satisfaction to His heart], the Lord said to Himself, I will never again curse the ground because of man, for the imagination (the strong desire) of man's heart is evil and wicked from his youth;

neither will I ever again smite and destroy every living thing, as I have done.

Genesis 8:20-21

All altars are places of exchange. Growing up in Africa, I noticed that each time our parents or grandparents took us to see a witch doctor to inquire from the gods, the witch doctors would demand some form of exchange on behalf of the idol. In one case, we were required to bring two chickens to the witch doctor before he would speak to us. After the exchange, the witch doctor would inquire from the idol (evil spirits) and tell us what we needed to do to get healed, prosper, get married, or have children. In some cases, the witch doctors would tell us how to destroy one of our enemies. Imagine - my pleasant surprise when I discovered that what African witch doctors were doing was based upon an ancient biblical pattern, except for the fact that as messengers of Satan, they had twisted the purpose of altars to serve the agenda of demons. I discovered that in the Bible, God made it very clear to the children of Israel that altars are places of exchange. In the above passage of scripture, Noah built an altar to the LORD, and he gave God an offering of *every clean [four-footed] animal and of every clean fowl or bird.* In exchange, God made a vow never to curse the ground because of man's wickedness nor destroy the Earth with a flood.

True to form, the devil is a master copycat. Who can blame him? Satan also demands an "exchange" from human attendants who have idols and evil altars in their souls or bloodline. Some people end up exchanging the "eternal security" of their soul for power, fame, and money in this life. Listen to what Satan told Jesus during His wilderness experience, according to Matthew 4:9., *"And the third time the accuser lifted Jesus up into a very high mountain range and showed him all the kingdoms of the world and all the splendor that goes with it. "All of these kingdoms I will give to you," the accuser said, "if only you will kneel down before me and worship me."* Until we get rid of the idols in our soul or bloodline, they will demand an exchange from us.

8.   All altars are places of covenant.

When they came to the place of which God had told him, Abraham built an altar there; then he laid the wood in order and bound Isaac his son and laid him on the altar on the wood. [15] The Angel of the Lord called to Abraham from heaven a second time [16] And said, I have sworn by Myself, says the Lord, that since you have done this and have not withheld [from Me] or begrudged [giving Me] your son, your only son, [17] In blessing I will bless you and in multiplying I will multiply your descendants like the stars of the heavens and like the sand on the seashore. And your Seed (Heir) will possess the gate of His enemies, [18] And in your Seed [Christ] shall all the nations of the earth be blessed and [by Him] bless themselves, because you have heard and obeyed My voice.

Genesis 22:9,15-18

All altars are places of agreement or covenants. They are places of meeting where humanity meets with divinity to enter into legal and covenantal agreements that are, in most cases, multi-generational. When Abraham demonstrated his total obedience and loyalty to God at an altar by his willingness to sacrifice his son, Isaac, God entered into a living covenant with him. We can definitely say that all covenants, whether they are righteous or evil, are sustained on and by altars. So, before you can break a demonic covenant over a person's life, it behooves you to understand the altar that the covenant stands on. Covenants are impossible to sustain without altars.

9. All altars can hear.

The man cried against the altar by the word of the Lord, O altar, altar, thus says the Lord: Behold, a son shall be born to the house of David, Josiah by name; and on you shall he offer the priests of the high places who burn incense on you, and men's bones shall be burned on you.

1 Kings 13:2

If I have learned anything from God, it is that there are no meaningless details in scripture. In the above scripture, a nameless prophet of God is sent to Bethel to prophesy against the altar in Bethel. In the prophecy, the prophet addressed the evil altar directly and said, *"O altar, altar, thus says the Lord: Behold, a son shall be born to the house of David, Josiah by name; and on you shall he offer the priests of the high places who burn incense on you, and men's bones shall be burned on you."* The million-dollar question is, *"why is he talking do an altar if the altar cannot hear his voice?"* The answer is profoundly simple; ***all altars can hear because all altars are kept alive by the supervising spirit behind them.***

All altars are alive, either through God's power or through the idol (demon-god) that powers the altar. When you're speaking to an altar, you are addressing God or the demon-god that the altar belongs to. That is precisely what God was doing through the nameless prophet. The Lord spoke to me and said, *"Francis, the evidence of hearing is an accurate response. If something has heard you then, it must do exactly what is asked of it."* So, what happened to the altar at Bethel that the prophet spoke to? It broke apart, and its ashes were poured out according to the word of the man of God. In other words, both the idol and the altar heard the word of the Lord. Katie Souza and I have prepared powerful prayers of activation in this book to help you demolish all the idols and evil altars in your soul and bloodline.

10. All altars either have God or an idol (demon-god) that is worshipped on the altar.

> *Then the Lord appeared to Abram and said, I will give this land to your posterity. So, Abram built an altar there to the Lord, who had appeared to him.*
>
> Genesis 12:7

> *Then Solomon built a high place for Chemosh the abominable idol of Moab, on the hill opposite Jerusalem, and for Molech the abominable idol of the Ammonites. [8] And he did so for all of his foreign wives, who burned incense and sacrificed to their gods.*
>
> 1 Kings 11:7

One of the things you must never forget is that ultimately altars are places of worship. **Worship is the number one activity of altars.** Why? Because we were created for God's pleasure. Worship is how we celebrate God and validate our allegiance and devotion to Him. Since the devil has always wanted to be like God, he ruthlessly demands worship from his followers. Because altars are places of worship, God declares emphatically, *"thou shall have no other gods before me!"* Coincidentally, this is the first commandment. So, when we have idols and the evil altars dedicated to them in our soul or bloodline, we will find ourselves worshiping demons instead of the

All altars are places of agreements or covenants

living God. That is why the message of this book is critical to the Body of Christ.

11. Spiritual warfare is the result of two opposing altars standing side by side.

The Philistines brought the ark of God from Ebenezer to Ashdod. *² They took the ark of God into the house of Dagon and set it beside Dagon [their idol]. ³ When they of Ashdod arose early on the morrow, behold, Dagon had fallen upon his face on the ground before the ark of the Lord. So, they took Dagon and set him in his place again.*

1 Samuel 5:1-2

I am confident every follower of Messiah-Jesus knows we are involved in high-stakes spiritual warfare between the kingdom of light and the forces of darkness. Recently, the Lord showed me that what we call "spiritual warfare" is nothing short of the *battle that ensues when an altar from God's Kingdom of light is placed* next to an altar from the kingdom of darkness. The close proximity and the fact that no two altars can occupy the same territory results in spiritual warfare. In the above passage of scripture, the Philistines brought the ark of God from Ebenezer to Ashdod. Upon their arrival, they took the ark of God into the house of Dagon, and they set the ark of God next to this demi-god idol.

When they woke up the following morning, Dagon was lying on the floor with his face looking at the ground. The ark of God, which was the altar of the Lord in Israel, was pronouncing its supremacy over the idol of the Philistines. Unfortunately, this same phenomenon takes place within the souls of believers who love the Lord Jesus but have idols in their soul they have yet to surrender to the LORD. They find themselves in constant spiritual turmoil in their will, mind, and emotions, as they struggle between the righteous demands of the altar of the Lord in their spirit and the evil desires of the idols and evil altars planted in their soul or bloodline. This book is a divine prescription for deliverance from this inner spiritual turmoil.

12. Whoever carries the superior altar takes the day!

But when they arose early the next morning, behold, Dagon had again fallen on his face on the ground before the ark of the Lord, and [his] head and both the palms of his hands were lying cut off on the threshold; only the trunk of Dagon was left him. [5] This is the reason neither the priests of Dagon nor any who come into Dagon's house tread on the threshold of Dagon in Ashdod to this day. [6] But the hand of the Lord was heavy upon the people of Ashdod, and He caused [mice to spring up and there was] very deadly destruction and He smote the people with [very painful] tumors or boils, both Ashdod and its territory. [7] When the men of Ashdod saw that it was so, they said, "The ark of the God of Israel must not remain with us, for His hand is heavy on us and on Dagon our god.

1 Samuel 5:4-7

According to the 12th Law of Altars, whoever carries the superior altar takes the day! What does this mean? It means that to be delivered from the power of an evil altar and the idol connected to it, we must strengthen the altar of the Lord in our life. *The altar of the Lord must become more potent than the idol and evil altar we want to destroy.* In the above passage of scripture, when the Philistines brought the ark of God into the house of Dagon, they did not understand the 12th Law of Altars. But God did! He did not waste time demonstrating to them, in no uncertain terms, that the altar of the ark of God was superior to the altar of the idol Dagon. When the Philistines found Dagon lying prostrate before the ark of God, they did not understand. So, they propped up the idol one more time and set it next to the ark of God. When they returned in the morning, the image of the idol Dagon was lying on the floor. This time, its head and both palms of its hands and feet were broken off its body! The Philistines got the message, and it terrified them!

The moral of the story is clear. *Whoever carries the superior altar takes the day!* For the LORD to deliver you from the power of the idols and evil altars erected in your soul or generational bloodline, you must make sure that you practice spiritual disciplines like worship, praying, fasting, reading, and studying the Word of God and so forth. Regular times of prayer and fasting will starve idols and evil altars in your soul while strengthening your spirit man to be more connected to the LORD. If the altar of sexual perversion in your life is stronger than the altar of sanctification, you'll lose the fight for holiness to the altar.

The Elijah Ministry: Rebuilding the Altar of the Lord

Then Elijah said to all the people, Come near to me. And all the people came near him. And he repaired the [old] altar of the Lord that had been broken down [by Jezebel]. [31] *Then Elijah took twelve stones, according to the number of the tribes of the sons of Jacob, to whom the word of the Lord came, saying, Israel shall be your name.* [32] *And with the stones Elijah built an altar in the name [and self-revelation] of the Lord.*

1 Kings 18:30-32

In closing, I want to teach you one of the master keys the LORD showed me on how to uproot and overthrow idols and the evil altars associated with them in your soul or bloodline. You must do what the prophet Elijah did when God used him to destroy the idol of Baal and the evil altars of the demi-god that Jezebel had erected all over Israel. Elijah repaired the broken altar of the LORD. He did this to teach us that the spirit world abhors a vacuum. When you uproot something demonic, you must replace it with its exact opposite and superior counterpart from the Kingdom of God. So, an altar of sexual perversion must be replaced by a righteous altar of holiness unto the LORD. After Elijah rebuilt the broken altar of the LORD, he essentially dethroned Baal from his exalted position in Israel and re-enthroned the LORD in Israel. As a result, the fire of the LORD fell from heaven and consumed everything on the altar. As you and I rebuild the broken altars of the LORD in our life, God's holy consuming fire will fall upon us and purify us from every form of spiritual defilement!

Whoever carries the
superior altar takes the
day!

Life Application Section

Memory Verse

Then Elijah said to all the people, Come near to me. And all the people came near him. And he repaired the [old] altar of the Lord that had been broken down [by Jezebel]. ³¹ Then Elijah took twelve stones, according to the number of the tribes of the sons of Jacob, to whom the word of the Lord came, saying, Israel shall be your name. ³² And with the stones Elijah built an altar in the name [and self-revelation] of the Lord. 1 Kings 18:30-32

Reflections

1. Write down three of the 12 Laws of Altars below

_____

_____

_____

_____

_____

_____

_____

2. Why did Elijah rebuild the broken altar of the LORD?

_____

_____

_____

Prayer of Release #3

The 12 Laws of Altars

"Heavenly Father, I ask for the Court of Heaven to be seated and the books to be opened as I come before the Judge of all the earth to plead my case so I can be justified and proven right. I am here in court with my official representative, the Holy Spirit, my advocate and counselor. Heavenly Father, I surrender all rights to self-representation; instead, I ask my defense attorney and mediator of the new covenant, the Lord Jesus Christ, to represent me in your Royal courtroom. Heavenly Father, I bring my case to your Supreme Court and to your Grace Court to face all charges and prosecute all idols and evil altars that are controlling my life and bloodline, in Jesus' Name. I am seeking deliverance from any soul wounds that have caused me to break the 12 Laws of Altars, and I am seeking a verdict of release from this Court.

I now enter a plea of 'guilty' into the court's records. The Bible says in Matthew 5:25, *"Come to terms quickly* [at the earliest opportunity] *with your opponent at law while you are with him on the way* [to court]*, so that your opponent does not hand you over to the judge, and the judge to the guard, and you are thrown into prison."*

Lord, since I am under oath, I cannot lie about my sinful activities and the iniquities of my bloodline that are connected to idolatry and erecting evil altars. I agree with any legitimate accusations brought by Satan against me and my bloodline. I submit a plea of guilty to all of Satan's charges connected to any kind of idolatry that my ancestors or I ever committed. I now formally submit my guilty plea to the court in Jesus' Name. It is also written: *And they overcame him by the blood of the Lamb and by the word of their testimony, and they did not love their lives to the death.* Revelation 12:11

As I testify on the witness stand, I first humbly repent of all the charges leveled against me so that I can overcome the enemy through the power of the blood and the word of my testimony. I repent of all personal and generational sin connected to becoming the human attendant to an evil altar. I repent for allowing a demonic spirit connected to an evil altar to be the guiding or supervising spirit over my life. I repent for empowering evil altars and the demon gods connected to them by sacrificing to them. I repent for allowing an evil altar to be my source of provision, supply, and fulfilment. I repent for repetitive destructive cycles of behaviors in my life that were connected to evil altars. I repent for allowing evil altars to speak and direct my life instead of being led by the Holy Spirit. I also repent for bringing any offering or sacrifice to an altar in exchange for any type of mental, emotional, or physical fulfillment. I repent for making agreements and covenants with any evil altar. I repent for erecting altars to demons instead of building an altar to worship the Lord. I repent for not speaking a word of judgment against evil altars that can hear my words and thus receive the judgment. I repent for worshipping demon gods connected to evil altars. I repent for allowing the evil altars in my soul to grow more powerful than the altar of the Lord. Heavenly Father, I place my sin and that of my ancestral bloodline under the blood of Jesus so I can overcome the enemy through my Redeemers blood in Jesus' Name.

As I continue to testify in this court, I also decree that I am under the power of the free and unmerited Grace of God. Since the Bible says it's impossible to keep the whole law, I need your redemptive grace. I decree that where my sin of idolatry has increased and abounded, Your

Grace has increased the more to overshadow my sin and even superabound over it. I also decree Galatians 2:21 over myself. It is written:

> *I do not ignore or nullify the [gracious gift of the] grace of God [His amazing, unmerited favor], for if righteousness comes through [observing] the Law, then Christ died needlessly. [His suffering and death would have had no purpose whatsoever.]"*

Heavenly Father, righteous Judge, I decree that because of the blood of Jesus and the power of His grace, I must be acquitted of all charges of attending to idols and evil altars in my life and bloodline. Because of the blood of Jesus Christ and grace, I must be acquitted of these charges of idolatry in Jesus' Name."

Now, Invite Jesus To Heal Your Soul!

Holy Spirit, I now invite you to search my soul (my will, mind, and emotions) and judge every idol and evil altar that causes my soul to violate the 12 Laws of Altars. I surrender every soul wound to you, Lord, for it's You who leads me beside the still waters and restores my soul. Lord Jesus, I am asking You to cleanse my soul with your blood, to cleanse my soul of every sin of idolatry, and to cleanse my soul of every evil altar that has been erected in my inner man. The Bible says it's the blood that atones for the soul. The Bible also declares that the blood cleanses my conscience; thus, I decree the blood is cleansing my mind right now of all thoughts connected to idolatry. I decree the blood is cleansing my will so that demon gods won't control it. I declare the blood is also cleansing my emotions to sever them from the control of idols and evil altars. Lord Jesus, I am asking You to also use your "Dunamis

Power" according to Acts 10:38 to heal every wound in my soul that the devil is using to oppress me. I also decree Ephesians 3:16 over myself that my soul is being strengthened and re-enforced by mighty Dunamis Power through the Holy Spirit. Thus, I am being strengthened in every place that my soul has been wounded through trauma so that the devil cannot use the pain of my trauma to drive me to idolatry. I also decree that mighty Dunamis Power is re-enforcing my soul to resist all temptations of idolatry. Finally, I decree and declare that I am full of the light of Christ and that my will, mind, and emotions are sound and fulfilling their office because my whole body is full of His light. I release the light of Christ into any darkness in my soul that came from idolatry, in Jesus' Name. So be it!

Right now, because my soul is being healed, I decree that I will never again be attendant to an evil altar. I declare that I will never allow a demonic spirit connected to an altar to be a guiding or supervising spirit over my life. I will never again bring sacrifices to an evil altar. I will never again be fed or provided by an evil altar. I will never again be stuck in a repetitive and destructive cycle connected to an evil altar. I will never again listen to the voice of an evil altar speaking to me and directing me. I will never again bring another sacrifice to an evil altar. I will never again make agreements and covenants with an evil altar. I will never fail to speak a word of divine judgment against an evil altar. I will never again lift my soul to an idol or demon spirit that is connected to an evil altar.

Loudly Declare These Supernatural Decrees So You Can Have Your Breakthrough

Heavenly Father

- I decree and declare that I am a godly attendant to the holy, righteous altar of God!

- I decree and declare that the Holy Spirit is my guiding and supervising the spirit.

- I decree and declare that I will only bring my sacrifices to the altar of the Lord.

- I decree and declare that I will only be fed and provided by the altar of the Lord.

- I decree and declare that I will repetitively and perpetually return to the altar of the Lord to worship for the rest of my life.

- I decree and declare that I will only listen to the voice of the Lord that comes from worshipping at His altar.

- I decree and declare that every exchange that I will ever make is godly and directed by the Holy Spirit.

- I decree and declare that I will only agree and cut covenants at the Altar of the Lord.

- I decree and declare that the altar of the Lord is listening to everything I am asking the LORD to do for me according to His will and riches in glory.

Time to Take Communion

Lord, as I take this communion, I do it in remembrance of You and Your victory on the cross and the resurrection. I decree that as I drink this cup of Your blood and eat Your body, my sins are forgiven, and my soul is nourished and refreshed and strengthened. I decree that as I eat Your flesh and drink Your blood, I will never be hungry and thirsty for idols again. I decree that as I partake of Your supper that my "Not Guilty" verdict from this Court concerning "setting up evil altars in my life and bloodline," will be sealed by the power and testimony of Your body and blood in Jesus' Name

4

Idols & Evil Altars in Your Soul

by

Katie Souza

"Little children keep yourselves from idols. Amen." 1 John 5:21 (KJV)

⊱⊱4⊰

IN OLD TESTAMENT times, people built physical altars out of stone or wood. Then those altars were dedicated to either God or the idols they served. Today, we erect these altars in our souls. The "soul" and not the spirit is the favorite hotel of idols. That is because your spirit-man never chases after idols. Once you are born again in Christ, your spirit-man becomes one with God. 1 Corinthians 6:17 says, *"But the person who is united to the Lord becomes one spirit with Him."* However, your soul is a different matter because it is not made perfect when you get saved like the spirit is. The soul, which is made up of the mind, will, and emotions, is a very fragile thing indeed. The Bible says the soul can literally get "wounded" through sin, traumas we experience, and ancestral bloodline iniquities. Look at this powerful verse, *"...the Lord binds up the hurt of His people and heals their wound [inflicted by Him because of their sins]."* Isaiah 30:26 (AMPC)

Sin of any kind can wound the soul. Once this happens, these "wounds" will control every part of your soul. These soul wounds will make you think wrong thoughts, make bad decisions, and experience unhealthy emotions. The Apostle Paul confirmed this phenomenon:

> *Now, if I do what I do not desire to do, it is no longer I doing it [it is not myself that acts], but the sin [principle] which dwells within me [fixed and operating in my soul].*

Romans 7:20 (AMPC)

Once your soul is wounded by sin, you will start doing crazy things you don't want to do! The Apostle Paul was a very godly man. And yet he was also controlled and manipulated by his wounded soul. Your soul can be your worst adversary until it gets healed by the grace and mercy of Jesus Christ. Sin, trauma, negative circumstances, or life's many storms can also wound your inner man and wreak havoc in your life. Job is an excellent example of this. He went through massive trauma. All of his flocks and herds were stolen in one day! Armed bandits killed his servants. He lost all of his children when a house collapsed on them. Add insult to injury; his body was also covered with painful boils. The Bible proves that these traumas wounded Job's soul. On 23 separate occasions, Job says things like, *"my soul is vexed, my soul is bitter, and my soul is poured out, all the while lamenting over the tragedies he endured."*

Knowing this, it becomes clear why the soul and not the spirit is attracted to idols. Your born-again spirit has been perfected in Christ Jesus. Your spirit never sins and can never be harmed by any crisis or the stresses you face in life. Notwithstanding, your soul-man is libel to injury of all kinds. Once the soul is wounded, it can cause you to have unhealthy desires for money, clothing, expensive cars, or whatever you've made into an idol. Why does this happen? Your wounded soul is continually searching for something to comfort and ease the pain you feel. Unfortunately, idols will strongly assert that they are the obvious cure for your misery even though it's a lie from the pit of hell!

Idols in Your Soul

Beloved, I implore you as aliens and strangers and exiles [in this world] to abstain from the sensual urges (the evil desires, the passions of the flesh, your lower nature) that wage war against the soul.

1 Peter 2:11

The wounds in your soul will drive you to idols to find relief from your suffering. This desire to self-medicate is the demonic doorway Satan uses to load you up with worthless idols. I know the feeling very well. While I was running wild on the streets as a criminal, there were times that my soul became oppressed. To combat the emotions I was feeling, I turned to food, alcohol, or dope to make me feel better. It didn't take long for these things to become my gods. When crazy people and traumatic situations stressed me out, a syringe full of speed, a bottle of Jägermeister, or a bag of Doritos with a can of bean dip always brought me the temporary satisfaction I was longing for. Most people, who eat like there is no tomorrow, are not gluttons; they are trying to medicate the excruciating agony they feel in their soul. The same goes for those who watch porn or have adulterous affairs. These outward sins are a sign something is wrong in their inner man. They have endured horrible situations, even things as traumatic as sexual molestation or losing a loved one. Then those tragedies left their souls wounded.

Maybe your soul got wounded in a messy divorce that scarred you so severely that you are constantly offended or depressed. Regrettably, this has led you to medicate yourself with excessive shopping sprees (on your ex's credit cards, no doubt lol). I know of devoted Christian parents who have been so traumatized by their children's sins of running the streets that they fell into alcoholism or prescription drug abuse to cope with their suffering. For some people, the idols that bring comfort to their wounded soul is food, movies, social media, or television. There is nothing wrong with any of these activities until they become excessive and undermine your time with the Lord. When this happens, you must realize that your soul is wounded and is driving you to break the first commandment, *"you shall have no other gods before Me."*

As someone who travels all over the world preaching the gospel, I know that Christians, and even pastors, are not exempt from the destructive power of idolatry. Some pastors have turned their church into an idol. They neglect their family's needs while fretting about their church's weekly attendance and offerings. Though they would never admit it, they are not really passionate about souls getting saved. They just want to make sure their church is the biggest, most popular, and wealthiest in their region. Idolatry has infected church leaders as well as their congregants.

I have fought many idols since getting out of prison and then overseeing a worldwide television outreach. I'm only a few years shy of 60, and being on high-definition television everyday challenges one's resolve not to turn their bathroom counter into a cosmetics altar! I know my sisters out there can relate. It's the idol called "our face!" Since I lead a worldwide television ministry, I am in dressing rooms and standing in front of TV cameras all the time. The pressure to look good is intense; so, before I knew it, beauty became my idol.

The Satisfaction of Idols is Only Temporary

Have you ever noticed that when you're feeling down or even desperate that you often eat to feel better or buy something to "fix" your feelings? Have you also taken note that though you may feel satisfied in the moment, the feeling soon fades away? Then you are right back to the miserable state you started with, howbeit with less money in your pocket. For me, it was food or the latest face cream that promised a wrinkle-free countenance that got to me. As soon as I placed the product in my shopping cart and made my purchase, I could feel a rush of instant gratification in my soul. Unfortunately, it was short-lived. The product always failed to live up to the hype.

These are the cycles that your wounded soul and idols can be an entrapment. Dr. Myles says, "*that all altars are places of perpetual or repetitive activity.*" You can always tell when your soul is wounded, and you've become addicted to idols. If you find yourself in a recurring cycle of inner pain, then medicating the pain with something or someone, only to feel extremely discouraged when the bandaid gets ripped off, then you are caught in the trap of idolatry. The devil wants to use your desperate

The wounds in your soul will drive you to idols to find relief from your suffering.

longing for comfort and fulfillment to ensnare you into a vicious cycle of idolatry and disappointment. If you see destructive recurring behaviors taking place in your life, it's because your soul is wounded and has become an altar for idols.

Only God Can Fulfill His Promises

I have also discovered that people run to their idols for comfort when God's promises have not yet manifested in their life. After prolonged periods of waiting for an answer, they turn to anti-depressants, medication, vitamins, and health supplements to cope. They soon become their idols. I have seen people who tried everything in the natural to lose weight but with no success. (I've witnessed dozens of weight loss miracles happening in my meetings, glory to God!) However, when the weight-loss breakthrough doesn't come fast enough, many end-up purchasing ineffective weight loss pills and join every fad diet they can find. Some even purchase exercise equipment, which eventually ends up in the garage, unused. A privileged few resort to spending thousands of dollars on surgeries in a desperate attempt to get the results they crave.

The more we run to our idols to get answers for our problems, instead of pressing into God to see His promises fulfilled, the more disillusioned we will become. The Bible is clear; idols will never bring the satisfaction they promise and are powerless to fulfill your prayers. Look what Psalm 115:5 says about this. *They idolize what they own and what they make with their hands, but their things can't talk to them or answer their prayers. Their possessions will never satisfy. Their futile faith in dead idols and dead works can never bring life or meaning to their souls.*

Idols cannot bring satisfaction to the pain in your soul, nor can they answer your prayers and bring you a miracle manifestation. Only God can do this. Many people don't realize that every time you run to idols to fulfill your petitions instead of waiting on God, you are inviting a demonic presence to delay your miracle even further! Don't forget that Psalm 106:36-37 says that idols are demon spirits. Thus, anything you make into an idol, be it possessions or people, will have a demonic presence that's attached to it. Look at what Jesus said about this.

> *I will not talk with you much more, for the prince (evil genius, ruler) of the world is coming. And he has no claim on Me. [He has nothing in common with Me; there is nothing in Me that belongs to him, and he has no power over Me.]*

John 14:30 (AMPC)

According to Jesus, Satan can only have power over you if you have something "in common" with him. Where is this *something-in-common* area found? Since your born-again spirit is perfect, your soul is the culprit. If you have sinned by pursuing idols, then you have created a landing strip in your soul for the devil to execute his will in your life. One of the definitions of an altar stated in this book by Dr. Myles is: "*An altar is a supernatural landing strip, a power station, a consecrated place, a place of exchange, where spirits (God, angels or demons) land, it is where humanity meets with divinity!*" Your wounded soul is the altar the enemy uses to control and devastate every part of your life. Dr. Myles also says, "*The Law of Dominion simply means that "spirits without physical bodies of dirt are illegal on earth"* unless they are functioning through a human." Spirits can't take dominion on this earth unless they operate through a human being. The only way they have the right to operate through you is if you have a wounded area in your soul that is "in common" with them. Then, and only then, can they work devastation in your life and work destruction in the earth.

Your Soul is the "In Common" Area

In Chapter One, I showed you how demonic spirits behind idols can cause you to be blind, deaf, dumb, and crippled in your body. They can also shut down your spiritual gifts, making it difficult to see in the spirit, hear the Lord's voice, speak accurate prophetic words, and walk uprightly with God. Now, I want to show you how your wounded soul is, what causes all this to happen to you. Do not forget what Paul said about spiritual gifts in 1 Cor 12:1-2 *"about the spiritual gifts ... 2 **You know that when you were heathens, you were led off after idols that could not speak...**"* Paul was making sure you knew that idols in your life would interfere with the gifts of the Spirit. Then he goes on a few verses later to tell you that your soul is the real problem,

> *Now there are distinctive varieties and distributions of endowments (gifts, extraordinary powers distinguishing certain Christians, due to the power of divine grace operating in their souls by the Holy Spirit) and they vary, but the [Holy] Spirit remains the same.*
>
> 1 Corinthians 12:4

Paul had just warned that idolatry would mess with the ministration of the gifts, but now he shows us the remedy for this problem, get our soul healed. When your soul is healed, you will demonstrate the *extraordinary powers distinguishing us from other Christians!* Some Christians believe that the gifts are all spiritual, but that is not true at all. Yes, the Holy Spirit distributes these gifts, but the more your soul is healed of all wounds, including those connected to idolatry, the more your gifts will explode. Would you like to walk in an extraordinary level of gifting? It only happens when you have God's divine power operating in and through your soul.

Extraordinary Gifts

I have been working on the healing of my soul for over a decade. Dr. Myles affectionately calls me the "Apostle of Soul Healing." Though I would never assume that title for myself, I have most definitely seen massive fruit of this revelation in my life, including in my administration of the supernatural gifts of the Spirit.

Over the last ten years of soul healing, my seer vision gift has become more exact and more accurate. Many of the visions I've received have led to incredible healing miracles. I also regularly hear words of knowledge from the Lord that do the same. More times than I can count, I've spoken a prophetic word that led to a major breakthrough in someone's life. My entire walk with God has been very supernatural. It's not because I am more holy than anyone else, but because I allowed God to heal the mess in my soul. Because He healed me, I can walk in the "extraordinary powers that distinguish certain Christians."

Idols in the Soul Affect Your Physical Body

Beloved, I pray that you may prosper in all things and be in health, just as your soul prospers.

3 John 2 (NKJV)

Your soul allows demonic powers to attack your physical body; this includes demonic forces behind the idols you worship. Blind Bartimaeus's father was Timaeus, a name which means to "defile oneself with idols." Idolatry starts when lust is birthed in our soul as we gaze upon a person or an object. Our eyes are the window to the soul. Whatever we behold, whether God or an idol, is what will imprint itself

85

on our inner man. In Bartimaeus's case, I believe he spent his life beholding all the idols his father brought into their house, and the result was his soul became wounded by that sin, and blindness was the result.

In the ninth chapter of Mark is the story of a little boy afflicted by an idolatrous spirit that made him deaf, dumb, and epileptic. According to Jesus, the child's soul provided that legal landing strip for this demonic power to assault him. The child's father pled with Jesus saying, *"But if You can do anything, do have pity on us and help us."* Jesus responded by saying, *"If you can believe, all things are possible to him who believes."* The word "possible" used in the text is "Dynatos," which, according to Thayer's Lexicon, means *strong in soul*. Jesus was telling the father that the healing of his child was possible once the little boy's soul was healed by the anointing Jesus carried.

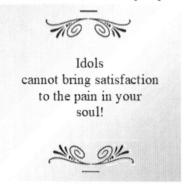

Idols cannot bring satisfaction to the pain in your soul!

Idols in your Bloodline are Carried in Your Soul

Bloodline idols in your soul can cause you to be crippled in your physical body. The man in Lystra was *"impotent in his feet, being a cripple from his mother's womb. He had never walked."* The word "impotent" used here is the Greek "adynatos," which has as its root in "dynatos," which again means *strong in soul*. This implies he was born with a wound in his soul passed down to him from his idol worshiping ancestors, causing him to be born crippled.

Soul wounds are generational and are often passed down to you while you are being formed in your mother's womb. When you were being knit together inside your mother, you received into your soul, all the generational iniquities and wounds of your ancestors. One proof of this is in the meaning of the word *"womb"* in the New Testament. It is the Greek word *"koilia."* It means ^*place where the fetus is conceived and nurtured until birth.* However, according to Thayer's Lexicon, it also means *the soul.* Why would the word "womb" also mean the soul? Because when you were being formed in the womb, your inner man received all the wounds and sins your ancestors had in their souls.

A Wounded Soul Leads to Food Idols

They are doomed and their fate is eternal misery (perdition); their god is their stomach (their appetites, their sensuality) and they glory in their shame, siding with earthly things and being of their party.

Philippians 3:19

It's your soul that allows demonic powers to drive you to lust after junk food and to overeat. Just recall what Paul said in 1 Cor 10:19-20. *"What do I imply then? That food offered to idols is [intrinsically changed by the fact and amounts to] anything or that an idol itself is a [living] thing? 20 No, I am suggesting that what the pagans sacrifice they offer [in effect] to demons (to evil spiritual powers) and not to God [at all]. I do not want you to fellowship and be partners with diabolical spirits [by eating at their feasts]."* When we keep running to the devil's table to feast, it causes us to agree with the demonic spirits that are behind these food idols. According to Paul, it's our soul that drives us to that table in the first place. Look at Paul's warning in Acts 15:29.

*Stay away from anything sacrificed to a pagan idol, from eating what is strangled or with any blood, and from any form of sexual immorality. You will be beautiful believers **if you keep your souls from these things**, and you will be true and faithful to our Lord Jesus."*

When your soul is wounded, it will continuously look for comfort and satisfaction. Regrettably, many times, food fits the bill. Excessive eating and drinking is a sign of a wounded soul. Gluttony unites us with these demon gods who always have food sacrificed to them. It's your soul that provides the 'in common" ground they need to control you and drive you to eat even more!

Binding the Strongman

Today, around the world, people still worship idols. In India alone, there are millions of gods encompassing everything from insects to cows. Here is why this fact is so important to us; who knows how many idols and demon gods your ancestors venerated going all the way back to Adam! What would happen if you had to name them all individually as you prayed to break them off of your bloodline? It would take a lifetime! Fortunately, you don't have to take on such a daunting task thanks to what the Bible has to say about binding the strongman.

But no one can go into a strong man's house and ransack his household goods right and left and seize them as plunder unless he first binds the strong man; then indeed he may [thoroughly] plunder his house.

Mark 3:27

One of the most powerful kingdom principles for capturing territory in the spirit world is the principle of binding the strongman. If we follow Jesus' advice, it will save us a lot of time trying to cast out low-level demons. Instead of working our way slowly up the ranks, we can legally start at the very top then quickly win the battle. By capturing the "strongman" that's in power over them all, it automatically destroys the power of all lower-ranked demons. I find this principle especially useful when it comes to overthrowing idols and evil altars in our soul or bloodline. Idolatry is one the easiest sins to commit by all humans, and there are millions of idols on earth, yet, we can take out every one of these idols in one swoop by binding the strongman first. And even better news, the Bible shows us that there is a strongman over every idol on this planet. His name is the Assyrian King.

> *For [the Assyrian] says, Are not my officers all either [subjugated] kings or their equal?... 10 As my hand has reached to the kingdoms of the idols [which were unable to defend them,] whose graven images were more to be feared and dreaded and more mighty than those of Jerusalem and of Samaria—11 Shall I not be able to do to Jerusalem and her images as I have done to Samaria and her idols? [says the Assyrian].*
>
> Isaiah 10:8, 10-11 (AMPC)

Jesus is called the King of kings. Here we see the Assyrian King making himself the demonic counterpart of that claim. In the dark realm, he is so powerful that he has other (demonic) kings subjected under his rule. These include all the demon gods that are behind the idols people worship. That is proven through his statement that all the other kingdoms' idols were unable to defend themselves against his rule. When I first read this, I couldn't stop shouting! The Holy Spirit had just given me a major key to quickly and effectively deal with every single idol in the history of the planet! Assyria was named as early as Genesis 2:14. It is an ancient spirit. When you bind this strongman, all the idols under him will have to bow and retreat!

One of the most powerful Kingdom principles for capturing territory in the spirit world is the principle of binding the strongman

The Soul and the Strong Man

The wounded soul is the landing strip for strongman spirits. Just look at the meaning of the word strongman (Greek "ischyros"), which, when referring to Satan, according to Strong's Concordance, means "strong, mighty." But it can also mean "one who has the strength of soul to sustain the attacks of Satan" (Thayer's Lexicon). So, to bind and defeat the strongman, you must have "strength of soul." As you are healed in your inner man, you will be able not only to resist his attack but also to exercise spiritual authority over him to bind him and thoroughly ransack all the spirits in his house.

This truth applies to you being empowered to defeat the Assyrian King, who is the strongman over all idols. Let's look at the proof from chapter 10 of Isaiah. *[The Lord] will consume the glory of the [Assyrian's] forest and of his fruitful field, both soul and body; and it shall be as when a sick man pines away or a standard-bearer faints.* Isaiah 10:18 (AMPC)

The Lord makes it clear that he is going to demolish all the destruction this strongman has planted in your life. Then the Lord tells us where Assyria's fruitful field lies; in *the soul and body!* This demonic king gets his legal right to attack you from the wounds and idolatry in your soul. He uses that "in common" area in your soul as his legal right to attack your physical body and the rest of your life. The good news is that when you become a strongman by being healed in your inner man, then his power over you will be broken.

Supernatural Powers to Heal Your Soul

God has provided for you to be healed through His Son Jesus Christ.

The Blood of Jesus

*For if with his weak conscience and his fears and semi-belief in the beings he has so recently rejected, he return to their shrines and take a part in their feasts, is it not likely that this will have an influence upon his mind, and work on him to his own destruction? 11... **and so defeat the very purpose of Christ's death, which was to free our weak minds and souls and consciences from idols**."*

1 Corinthians 8:10-11 GWC

According to this verse, the very purpose of Christ's death was to free your soul from idols! This is so powerful. Idolatry shipwrecks our relationship and intimacy with the Father. It is the number one sin that God commanded us to shun! So, of course, God would send His only Son to die for our idolatry so we could be free of their scourge. The blood Jesus shed at the cross has the power to cleanse our wounded souls of every sin connected to the worship of these demon gods. Leviticus 17:11 says, *"For the life of the flesh is in the blood, and I have given it to you upon the altar to make atonement for your souls; for it is the blood that makes atonement for the soul.'*

91

In ancient times, God's people sacrificed spotless animals then put the blood on the altar of the Lord to atone for their sin. Sin lives in the soul. Today your soul is an altar that either worships God or idols. When you plead the Blood of Jesus over the altar of your soul, then it will be cleansed of its idolatrous worship. As you repent for the idols in your life and those in your bloodline, the blood will wipe out the record of idolatry in your history, taking away the legal right those demonic powers have to torment and afflict you. *Evil alters in our life are landing strips for idols to land. They are wounds in our souls- "in common with"*

Communion

One of the most potent ways to partake of the cleansing power of the blood of the cross is by participating in the Lord's supper. The Bible says as we do so, we do it in *remembrance"* of Him and what He accomplished for us at Calvary. Don't forget that 1 Corinthians 8 says that the purpose of Christ's death was to free our souls from idols! That is why you must take communion and do it often, even excessively. Without partaking of communion, you will not have total victory over these evil altars in your soul. Communion heals your soul. Look at the proof in Matthew 26:27 where Jesus said, *"And he took the cup, and gave thanks, and gave it to them, saying, Drink ye all of it;*[28] *For this is my blood of the new testament, which is shed for many for the remission of sins."*

The word "drink" used here (Greek word Pino) means, "to receive into the soul what serves to refresh, strengthen, and nourish it unto life eternal." Thus, every time you partake of His cup, your soul gets refreshed in every place it's weary, and then strengthened in every area that is wounded. It is also nourished in every area where it is weak. Through communion, your soul will become so strong that it won't run to any idols for comfort anymore. Communion comes directly against the demon spirits that are driving you to drugs, alcohol, food addictions, and so forth. Look at what Jesus said in John 6 when he admonished his followers to "eat His flesh and drink His blood." *And Jesus said unto them, I am the bread of life: he that cometh to me shall never hunger; and he that believeth on me shall never thirst. John 6:35*

Believe it or not, this verse contains powerful soul healing instructions. The word *thirst* (dipsaō), according to Thayer's Lexicon, means "those who are said to thirst, who painfully feel their want of, and eagerly long for those things by which the soul is refreshed, supported, and strengthened." The wounded soul is incessantly hungry and thirsty. A wounded person often finds themselves going from one fix to the next, feasting upon each idol but never able to quench their thirst. That is why we must run to Jesus and His table! He promises that when you do so that you will never hunger and thirst again! His body and blood will cause your soul to be totally refreshed, supported, and strengthened.

The good news is that you can apply this truth specifically to the idols in your soul that are driving your negative food habits and unhealthy weight gain. Do you remember what Paul said about fellowshipping with diabolical spirits by "eating at their feasts"? Well, look at what Paul stated just a few verses earlier.

Therefore, my dearly beloved, shun (keep clear away from, avoid by flight if need be) any sort of idolatry (of loving or venerating anything more than God)...[16] *The cup of blessing [of wine at the Lord's Supper] upon which we ask [God's] blessing, does it not mean [that in drinking it] we participate in and share a fellowship (a communion) in the blood of Christ (the Messiah)? The bread which we break, does it not mean [that in eating it] we*

> *participate in and share a fellowship (a communion) in the body of Christ?*
>
> 1 Cor 10:145, 16 (AMPC)

How do you break the fellowship you have with demonic spirits that came from eating at their feasts? You participate in and share a fellowship in the blood and body of Christ! Communion reverses the effects these demonic gods have on your soul: this includes you being loosed from the strongman behind it all, the Assyrian king. Once you are free from his tyranny, then his ability to drive you to eat too fast, overeat, consume junk food, and sugars will be crushed. Communion even takes away those demonic hunger pains. After all, Jesus said my flesh is meat, indeed, and my blood is drink indeed. (John 6:55)

I want to insert a quick story here. My whole life, I have always eaten very fast. In prison, that behavior went deeper into my soul as they only give you a few minutes at chow to finish your meal. I knew this was not healthy for my body and even created demonic connections to my life. One day I was proven right. I asked God if there was a demonic presence behind me gulping down my food, and immediately, I saw a vision of a scarf wrapped around my neck. Curious, I looked up the word "scarf" and was shocked at what I found, "To eat or drink voraciously; devour" (free dictionary). Yikes! As I reread the definition, the Holy Spirit downloaded to me the spirit behind my scarfing. It was the Assyrian King! The Bible says this;

> *And it shall be in that day that the burden of [the Assyrian] shall depart from your shoulders, and his yoke from your neck. The yoke shall be destroyed because of fatness [which prevents it from going around your neck].*

Isaiah 10:27 (AMPC)

The Assyrian's evil yoke was wrapped around my neck, making

Communion reverses the effects these demonic gods have on your soul!

me scarf down my food! That's when I decided to take communion five times a day and soak in the power of the anointing until that behavior was broken off of me. It didn't take very long before the fellowship I had built with diabolical spirits by eating at their feasts was totally severed!

The Holy Spirit and Dunamis Power

How God anointed and consecrated Jesus of Nazareth with the [Holy] Spirit and with strength and ability and power; how He went about doing good and, in particular, curing all who were harassed and oppressed by [the power of the devil, for God was with Him.

Acts 10:38

The word "power" in Acts 10:38 comes from the Greek word "Dunamis." It means "the power to perform miracles and excellence of soul." The Bible says you will receive "power" (Dunamis) when the Holy Spirit comes upon you. Thus, as a born-again believer, you have an endless supply of soul healing power inside of you. So, whether you get angry, offended, or have gone through a trauma that's wounded your soul, you can be healed by the Holy Spirit and the "Dunamis" power that's inside of you.

95

Notice that verse in Acts says that Jesus was "anointed" with this Dunamis power. That's what Dunamis is, an anointing that God puts in you to help you break free of every demonic oppression, including that of the Assyrian King. Earlier, you saw how Isaiah 10 says, "the anointing breaks the yoke." Well, I want you to look at that verse again in the Amplified Classic version because it specially says the anointing will break the yoke of the Assyrian king off your neck!

> *And it shall be in that day that the burden of [the Assyrian] shall depart from your shoulders, and his yoke from your neck. The yoke shall be destroyed because of fatness [which prevents it from going around your neck].*
>
> Isaiah 10:27 (AMPC)

I often hear people quoting this verse. They enthusiastically say, "the anointing breaks the yoke!" However, few connect this truth in Isaiah with the fact that this anointing breaks the yoke of the Assyrian King off your life! Don't forget that Dunamis makes your soul excellent! When the anointing heals your inner man, then you will have nothing in you that's in common with Assyrian and his army of idols so that they won't have any power over you. When I prayed for my friend John Blake to be freed from that Egyptian idol and the elevated ammonia it put on his body, I simply asked the Holy Spirit to fill his soul with Dunamis power. I knew that the anointing of Dunamis would heal him, cause him to have nothing in common with that spirit, then break the yoke of that devil and its sickness off his life. You can pray the same way and receive amazing results as I did.

The Apostle Paul prayed for your soul to be healed by Dunamis power. Look at his powerful decree.

> *May He grant you out of the rich treasury of His glory to be strengthened and reinforced with mighty power in the inner man by the [Holy] Spirit [Himself indwelling your innermost being and personality].*
>
> Ephesians 3:16

The "mighty power" Paul spoke of here is Dunamis. Notice he says it would strengthen and reinforce your "inner man." He is not referring to your born-again spirit as it is perfect in Christ and needs no help. Instead, he is saying that your soul will be strengthened and reinforced in every area where it is weak through the action of the Holy Spirit: this includes healing your inner man and making it resistant to the temptation of idolatry.

Light of Christ

Jesus called himself "the Light of the World" (John 8:12)t refer). Then He went on to say that whoever believed in Him would not have to walk in darkness but have the light which brings life! The light that streams from Jesus's radiance is not just there to make him look good. It is a power that can change and heal your soul. Look at the powerful proof in Luke 11:

> *"Your eye is the lamp of your body; when your eye (your conscience) is sound and fulfilling its office, your whole body is full of light; but when it is not sound and is not fulfilling its office, your body is full of darkness. Be careful, therefore, that the light that is in you is not darkness. If then your entire body is illuminated, having no part dark, it will be wholly bright [with light], as when a lamp with its bright rays gives you light."*

Luke 11:34(AMPC)

The eye is the window to the soul. Here, Jesus tells you how each part of your soul can become *"sound and fulfilling its office."* It happens when *"your whole body is full of light."* Your mind, will, and emotions were created by God to hold particular offices in your inner man and perform specific duties. Your mind was designed to rightly divide good thoughts from bad, have healthy powers of reasoning, and operate with a clean, creative imagination. The job of your will is to make spirit-led decisions, instead of being directed and controlled by the pain of your wounds and the demons behind the idols connected to your soul. Your emotions were also created by God to be sound and at peace. You were created to have God-given emotions with healthy reactions to the most trying and difficult circumstances. According to Jesus, every part of your soul will be sound and properly fulling its office when your whole body is filled with Christ's light.

Jesus' light is a power that heals anything in your soul that is in common with idols and strongmen like the Assyrian king. In Isaiah 10, God speaks another judgment against that Strongman, and he connects it to the light of Christ healing of men's souls and bodies whom Assyria has taken captive.

> *And the Light of Israel shall become a fire and His Holy One a flame, and it will [a]burn and devour [the Assyrian's] thorns and briers in one day.* [18] *[The Lord] will consume the glory of the [Assyrian's] forest and of his fruitful field, both soul and body; and it shall be as when a sick man pines away or a standard-bearer faints.*

Isaiah 10:17-18 (AMPC)

Notice the word "Light" here is capitalized. That means its Jesus, and the light radiates from Him. The Lord judges the Assyrian's fruit field in your soul and body by releasing the blazing light of his Son to heal you. (Please read chapter 7 of my book <u>Be Revived; Defeating the Spirit of Death with the Power of Life</u>). An example in the New Testament of the Light of Jesus healing someone afflicted in soul and body by an idolatrous spirit is again in the deaf and dumb child's story. His deliverance happened right after Jesus descended from the mount of transfiguration, where the Bible says Jesus's *appearance changed in their presence, and His face shone clear and bright like the sun, and His clothing became as white as light.* and *a shining cloud [composed of light] overshadowed them. (*Matthew 17:2, 5 AMPC*).* Jesus had been overshadowed and filled with light from the presence of the Father, and I believe this facilitated the deliverance of that child. Why do I say that? Because the Bible made a point of saying that same light was still on Jesus as he healed that demon-possessed boy.

> "*...when they saw Jesus [<u>returning from the holy mount, His face and person yet glistening</u>]... </u>*[17]*And one of the throng replied to Him, Teacher, I brought my son to You, for he has a dumb spirit.*

> Mark 9:15, 17 (AMPC)

I encourage you to look up every scripture with the word light in it and daily decree it over yourself. <u>The more you sit in the presence of Christ in worship and adoration of Him and His Word, the more His light</u> <u>will fill you, heal you, and free you of every demon god that has taken you captive.</u>

Life Application Section

Memory Verse

*Stay away from anything sacrificed to a pagan idol, from eating what is strangled or with any blood, and from any form of sexual immorality. You will be beautiful believers **if you keep your souls from these things**, and you will be true and faithful to our Lord Jesus."* Acts 15:29

Reflections

1. Can the iniquities and soul wounds of previous generations be transferred to children in the womb? If so, how?

_____

_____

_____

_____

2. What makes the wounded soul easily lift itself up to idols?

_____

_____

_____

_____

_____

_____

_____

Prayer of Release #4

Overthrowing Idols and Evil Altars

"Heavenly Father, I ask for the Court of Heaven to be seated and the books to be opened as I come before the judge of all the earth to plead my case so I can be justified and proven right. I am here in court with my official representative, the Holy Spirit, my advocate and counselor. Heavenly Father, I surrender all rights to self-representation; instead, I ask my defense attorney and mediator of the new covenant, the Lord Jesus Christ, to represent me in your Royal Courtroom. Heavenly Father, I bring my case to your Supreme Court and to your Grace Court to face all charges and prosecute all idols and evil altars that are controlling my life and bloodline, in Jesus' Name. I am seeking deliverance from any soul wounds that I have in common with demonic spirits behind idols and evil altars and a verdict of release from this Court.

I now enter a plea of 'guilty' into the court's records. The Bible says in Matthew 5:25, *"Come to terms quickly* [at the earliest opportunity] *with your opponent at law while you are with him on the way* [to court]*, so that your opponent does not hand you over to the judge, and the judge to the guard, and you are thrown into prison."*

Lord, since I am under oath, I cannot lie about my sinful activities and the iniquities of my bloodline that are connected to idolatry and erecting evil altars. I agree with any legitimate accusations brought by Satan against me and my bloodline. I submit a plea of guilty to all of Satan's charges connected to any kind of idolatry that my ancestors or I ever committed. I now formally submit my guilty plea to the court in

Jesus' Name." It is also written: *And they overcame him by the blood of the Lamb and by the word of their testimony, and they did not love their lives to the death.* Revelation 12:11

As I testify on the witness stand, I first humbly repent of all the charges leveled against me so that I can overcome the enemy through the power of the blood and the word of my testimony. I repent of all personal and generational sins that wounded my soul that are connected to idols and altars. I repent for being controlled by the wounds in my soul that were driving me to pursue idols. I repent for chasing after my idols to find satisfaction and comfort my wounded soul. I repent for running to idols to try to fulfill the promises I received from God instead of waiting on the Lord to fulfill my promises. I repent for anything and everything that I have in common in soul with idols. I repent for everything in my soul that is suppressing my spiritual gifts and blocking me from walking in extraordinary powers that distinguish certain Christians. I repent for anything in my soul that is blocking the healing and health of my physical body and finances. I repent for any generational soul wound that has been carried in my bloodline. I repent for not keeping my soul from food idols. I repent for any wound in my soul that is connected to the strongman having power over me. Heavenly Father, I place my sin and that of my ancestral bloodline under the blood of Jesus so I can overcome the enemy through my redeemers' blood. In Jesus' Name.

As I continue to testify in this court, I also decree that I am under the power of the free and unmerited Grace of God. Since the Bible says it's impossible to keep the whole law, I need your redemptive grace. I decree that where my sin of idolatry has increased and abounded, Your Grace has increased the more to overshadow my sin and even superabound over it. I also decree Galatians 5:4 over myself. It is written:

If you seek to be justified and declared righteous and to be given a right standing with God through the Law, you are brought to nothing and so separated (severed) from Christ. You have fallen away from grace (from God's gracious favor and unmerited blessing).

Heavenly Father, Righteous Judge, I decree that because of the blood of Jesus and the power of His grace I must be acquitted of all charges of allowing my soul to be wounded through my sins of idolatry and the erecting of evil altars in my soul and bloodline. Because of the blood of Jesus Christ and grace, I must be acquitted of all these charges of idolatry in Jesus' Name."

Now, Invite Jesus To Heal Your Soul!

Holy Spirit, I now invite you to search my soul (my will, mind, and emotions) and judge every idol and evil altar that causes my soul to window shop for idols. I surrender every soul wound to you, Lord, for its You, who leads me beside the still waters and restores my soul. Lord Jesus, I am asking You to cleanse my soul with your blood, to cleanse my soul of every sin of idolatry, and to cleanse my soul of every evil altar that has been erected in my inner man. The Bible says it's the blood that atones for the soul. The Bible also declares that the blood cleanses my conscience; thus, I decree the blood is cleansing my mind right now of all thoughts connected to idolatry. I decree the blood is cleansing my will so that demon gods won't control it. I declare the blood is also cleansing my emotions to sever them from the control of idols and evil altars. Lord Jesus, I am asking You to also use your "Dunamis Power" according to Acts 10:38, to heal every wound in my soul that the devil uses to oppress me. I also decree Ephesians 3:16 over myself that my soul is being strengthened and re-enforced by mighty Dunamis Power through the Holy Spirit. Thus, I am being strengthened in every place that my soul has been wounded through trauma, so that the devil cannot use the pain of my trauma to drive me to idolatry. I also decree that mighty Dunamis Power is re-enforcing my soul to resist all temptations of idolatry. Finally, I decree and declare that I am full of the light of Christ and that my will, mind, and emotions are sound and fulfilling their office because my whole body is full of His light. I release the light of Christ into any darkness in my soul that came from idolatry, in Jesus' Name, so be it!

Right now, because my soul is being healed, I decree that my soul is no longer controlled by any wounds that are used to drive me to pursue idols. I decree that my soul is so healed that I no longer need to find satisfaction and comfort from idols. I decree that I trust the Lord totally, and my soul will patiently wait for Him to fulfill His promises. I decree I have nothing in my soul in common with the demon gods connected to idols or any evil altar. I decree that my soul is filled with divine power to cause me to walk in the extraordinary gifts of the Holy Spirit. I decree that I am prospering in my finances and physical health even as my soul prospers. I decree that my soul is healed of all generational soul wounds that used to be in my bloodline. I decree that my soul is healed of every wound connected to food idols. I decree I have nothing in my soul that is in common with the strongman over idols and evil altars, in Jesus' Name, I pray.

Loudly Declare These Supernatural Decrees So You Can Have Your Breakthrough

Heavenly Father

- I decree and declare that my relationship with God will explode and cause exponential blessings to be released in my life because my soul is not lusting after idols.

- I decree and declare that from this moment on, my soul is filled with supernatural peace, joy, and satisfaction. I am content in every situation, no matter my circumstances.

- I decree and declare that as I wait on God alone, His promises will fully manifest in every single area of my life.

- I decree and declare that I have authority over every demon god, every evil altar, and every strongman over idols because I have nothing in my soul that is common with them.

- I decree and declare that I will operate in high levels of gifting in prophecy, word of knowledge, discerning of spirits, the working of miracles.

- I decree and declare that because I have prosperity of soul, that financial gifts, blessings, business opportunities, and favor with man and God are continually flowing in my direction.

- I decree and declare that because I have prosperity of soul, every part of my physical body is experiencing divine health. I have no disease, no disorder, no sickness, no virus, no harmful bacteria, no tumors, no cancer, no arthritis, no skeletal or muscular diseases, no respiratory diseases, no circulatory diseases, or reproductive diseases, no blood diseases, no nerve disorders.

- I decree and declare that because I have prosperity of soul that I have full control over my food consumption. I only desire healthy food. I never lust after junk food, fast food, or sugars. I have access to supernatural weight loss, and I live at my perfect body weight, in Jesus' Name, Amen.

Time to Take Communion

Lord, as I take this communion, I do it in remembrance of You and Your victory on the cross and the resurrection. I decree that as I drink this cup of Your blood and eat Your body, my sins are forgiven, and my soul is nourished and refreshed and strengthened. I decree that as I eat Your flesh and drink Your blood, I will never be hungry and thirsty for idols again. I decree that as I partake of Your supper that my "Not Guilty" verdict from this Court concerning "setting up evil altars in my life and bloodline," will be sealed by the power and testimony of Your body and blood in Jesus' Name

THE IDOLS ARE RIOTING

Taking Idols to the Courts of Heaven

by

Katie Souza

[You idols made by men's hands, prove your divinity!] Produce your cause [set forth your case], says the Lord. Bring forth your strong proofs, says the King of Jacob.

Isaiah 41:21 (AMPC)

THERE ARE two main areas in your life that these demon gods use to get their legal rights against you, namely:

3. In the soul and,
4. In the Courts of Heaven

We have already looked at the soul. Now let's investigate how Satan gets his legal rights to destroy your life by accusing you in the Courts of Heaven. Satan may have been kicked out of heaven, but he still has access to its court system. Allow me to offer the scripture below as proof.

> *Then I heard a strong (loud) voice in heaven, saying, Now it has come—the salvation and the power and the kingdom (the dominion, the reign) of our God, and the power (the sovereignty, the authority) of His Christ (the Messiah); for the accuser of our*

brethren, he who keeps bringing before our God charges against them day and night, has been cast out!

Revelation 12:10

Satan accuses us before God day and night. The word "accuser," according to Thayer's Greek Lexicon, is the word "katēgoreō," which means "to make accusations before a judge." This proves that the place Satan files "charges" against us is in the heavenly courts. No allegation can have binding ramifications resulting in punishment unless it is presented in a court of law. This is why Satan doesn't just shake his fist at you when he is indicting you of sin. Instead, he brings every accusation before God in Heaven's courtroom so he can get a legal judgment against you. This judgment then gives him the ability to inflict some sort of punishment upon your life.

God is called "Judge of all the earth," over 76 times in the Bible. According to the Bible, He enforces His just laws from the Courts of Heaven. *"You caused judgment to be heard from heaven; The earth feared and was still, When God arose to judgment, to deliver all the oppressed of the earth."* Psalm 76:8-9 (NJKV*)*

God's judgments are so perfect that the decrees released from His court can deliver every oppressed person in the earth no matter what has them bound. However, to receive a favorable verdict from the court, you must show up to face the accusations the enemy has filed against you. Did you know that when there is a court case between two people or entities, whoever doesn't show up for court loses? I know this fact more than most because of my past as a career criminal. I was arrested quite often. And every time, I would post bail with the promise of returning to court. However, when I failed to appear, the court would issue a warrant for my arrest. When the police detained me again, I was promptly taken back to court, and it wasted no time in sentencing me to a lengthy jail sentence. Moral of the story; whoever doesn't show up for court loses!

Even God instructs us to come to court to face the charges Satan has filed against us. *Put Me in remembrance [remind Me of your merits]; let us plead and argue together. Set forth your case, that you may be justified (proved right).* Isaiah 43:26 (AMPC)

In the above passage, God issues a command that you must come before His holy bench to present your case. Why? So, you can be proven right and the devil wrong – based upon the finished work of Jesus! That's the beautiful thing about going into the Courts of Heaven. You will always be found innocent! Not because of your righteousness, which is as filthy rags, but because of the blood, mercy, and grace of our Lord Jesus Christ!

Jesus Healed Souls and Took Devils to Court

When it comes to getting free from any demonic spirit, including spirits behind idols, you must first get your soul healed of everything you have in common with them. But in addition to this, you must also take these devils to court. Whenever Jesus freed people of demonic oppression and sickness, He did it by operating in both realms. Look at this incredible example in Luke 13:10-13:

"Now He was teaching in one of the synagogues on the Sabbath. And behold, there was a woman who had a spirit of infirmity eighteen years, and was bent over and could in no way raise herself up. But when Jesus saw her, He called her to Him and said to her, 'Woman, you are loosed from your infirmity.' And He laid His hands on her, and immediately she was made straight, and glorified God."

The spirit of infirmity used two areas as legal grounds to attack this woman and bend her spine over. First, let's look at the demonic landing strip that was in her soul. In the passage, Jesus uses the word "infirmity" (from the Greek word "astheneia") to describe the demon that was bending her spine. The term "infirmity" (astheneia) means "weakness and infirmity of body and soul," according to Thayer's Greek Lexicon. By definition, this woman had an unhealed area in her soul that was giving the spirit of infirmity the right to attack her body. I don't know if it was from idolatry in her bloodline because, after all, idols cant walk or if it was trauma or some other issue. Nevertheless, whichever way we slice her condition, she had something in her soul that was "in common" with the spirit afflicting her.

How did Jesus fix her soul issue? The Bible says He "laid hands" on her and made her straight. When Jesus touched her, He transferred upon her the anointing of "Dunamis" that He was carrying, according to Acts 10:38. Once again, "Dunamis" means "excellence of soul." Consequently, we know Jesus healed her of the wound in her inner man that had been giving the devil access to her life.

So Jesus healed her soul, but then he didn't stop there. He also took the spirit of infirmity that was afflicting her into the Courts of Heaven. He declared over her, *"Woman, you are loosed from your infirmity."* The word "loose," according to Thayer's Greek Lexicon, is "apolyō." In Greek, it means "to acquit one accused of a crime and set him at liberty!" When Jesus said, "You are loosed," to the woman, He went in the spirit to the Courts of Heaven and got her acquitted of the crime Satan had accused her of! Once she was cleared of all "charges in the heavenly courts," and Jesus' Dunamis power healed her soul, then she was totally free! Hallelujah!

Heal the Soul & Go to Court!

People used to say to me, "Katie, you just have to take people into the Courts of Heaven. You don't have to do that soul healing stuff!" My response was always immediate, "I don't believe that at all. I've seen too many miracles happen to people after they got their soul healed." The story of the woman bound with a spirit of infirmity provides biblical proof that we need to do soul healing along with going into the Courts of Heaven. Jesus did both "works," so we need to follow His perfect example.

In the Courts of Heaven you are always found innocent!

Jesus told us to take Satan to Court

Jesus instructs us to take the devil to court in the story of the persistent widow and the corrupt judge.

> *"ALSO [Jesus] told them a parable to the effect that they ought always to pray and not to turn coward (faint, lose heart, and give up). He said, 'In a certain city there was a judge who neither reverenced and feared God nor respected or considered man. And there was a widow in that city who kept coming to him and saying, Protect and defend and give me justice against my adversary. And for a time he would not; but later he said to himself, "Though I have neither reverence or fear for God nor respect or consideration for man, Yet because this widow continues to bother me, I will defend and protect and avenge her, lest she give me intolerable annoyance and wear me out by her*

continual coming or at the last she come and rail on me or assault me or strangle me." Then the Lord said, 'Listen to what the unjust judge says! And will not [our just] God defend and protect and avenge His elect (His chosen ones), who cry to Him day and night? Will He defer them and delay help on their behalf? I tell you, He will defend and protect and avenge them speedily. However, when the Son of Man comes, will He find [persistence in] faith on the earth?'"

Luke 18:1-8

The persistent widow kept coming to the unrighteous judge to receive justice from her "adversary," which is a derivative of the Greek word "antidikos," which means "an opponent (in a lawsuit); specifically, Satan!" The word is made up of two Greek words, "anti" and "dikos." Anti means "against" and "dikos" means rights. Thus, this means that Satan is an "antidikos," an adversary who is working against your legal rights. He does this by being your "opponent in a lawsuit" as the meaning of antidikos suggests. Since Jesus told this story as a parable, it indicates that Satan is filing lawsuits against all of us right now in the Courts of Heaven. He is our opponent in court, and we must be persistent, like the widow, to not only appear before the Righteous Judge but to go repeatedly, until we get the justice we need! In my gangster days, I would say it this way, "shoot and keep shooting until that sucker is dead!" Without this type of prevailing mentality that takes no prisoners, we will not win the battle against the demons behind the idols we battle with every day.

Idols Riot

Satan is the accuser of the brethren. He goes into the Courts of Heaven to charge you with breaking God's law. Well, guess what?! The first and second commandment declares, *"you are to have no other gods before Me* and *do not make for yourself any graven images!"* The most significant and most frequent accusation the enemy will bring against you in court is about your idols.

Let me tell you about the time God revealed to me that I needed to take my idols to court. I had spent years battling them and had seen huge breakthroughs manifest in my life by getting my soul healed. However, I couldn't seem to totally break free of the remaining stranglehold they had on me. One day, in total frustration, I asked God what the heck was going on! He immediately answered with this strange statement, "The idols are rioting." I couldn't figure out what He meant. So, I googled the phrase and was shocked by what I discovered. The phrase *"Idols Riot"* was connected to the story of Paul's time in Ephesus and how a riot broke out when the city's idol worshiping citizens tried to stop Paul from preaching against their culture of idolatry.

The riot was triggered by a silversmith named Demetrius, who brought a public complaint against Paul and his teachings.

But as time went on, there arose no little disturbance concerning the Way [of the Lord]. [24] *For a man named Demetrius, a silversmith, who made silver shrines of [the goddess] Artemis [Diana], brought no small income to his craftsmen.* [25] *These he called together, along with the workmen of similar trades, and said, Men, you are acquainted with the facts and understand that from this business we derive our wealth and livelihood.* [26] *Now you notice and hear that not only at Ephesus but almost all over [the province of] Asia this Paul has persuaded and induced people to believe his teaching and has alienated a considerable company of them, saying that gods that are made with human hands are not really gods at all. [27] Now there is danger not merely that this trade of ours may be discredited, but also that the temple of the great goddess Artemis may come into disrepute and count for nothing, and that her glorious magnificence may be degraded and fall into contempt—she whom all [the province of] Asia and the wide world worship. [28] As they listened to this, they were filled with rage and they continued to shout, Great is Artemis of the Ephesians!"*

Acts 19:23-28

Demetrius and his fellow tradesmen weren't going to let anything stop them from profiting from the making and selling of their idolatrous shrines. Demetrius' speech was so persuasive he managed to stir up his fellow tradesmen into a demonic frenzy. The Bible says that as they listened to Demetrius, *they were filled with rage, and they continued to shout, "Great is Artemis of the Ephesians!"* A riot ensued as the idol-worshiping people of Ephesus fiercely defended their goddess. The entire city began to shout as they rushed into the amphitheater. *The mob was out for blood!* They even dragged along with them Gaius and Aristarchus, Paul's ministry partners! Paul wanted to speak to the people to calm them down, but the disciples would not permit it out of fear for his life. When a man named Alexander attempted to bring peace in the midst of the riot, the mob just got more incensed. The Bible says, "*...as soon as they saw him and recognized that he was a Jew, a shout went up from them as the voice of one man, as for about two hours they cried, Great is Artemis of the Ephesians!* Acts 19:34

Wow! The entire city shouted praises to their goddess for two hours straight! Sadly, we can't even get Christians to praise God for two-minutes, much less for two hours! Interestingly, the Bible says the people of the city screamed with *the voice of one man!* I believe the evil spirits they idolized controlled them 100%, uniting them as one unit and driving them into a frenzied riot. The people were literally possessed! No one could stop them, that is until a representative from the city courts arrived. Look at what happened next.

> *And when the town clerk had calmed the crowd down, he said, Men of Ephesus, what man is there who does not know that the city of the Ephesians is guardian of the temple of the great Artemis and of the sacred stone [image of her] that fell from the sky? 36 Seeing then that these things cannot be denied, you ought to be quiet (keep yourselves in check) and do nothing rashly. 37 For you have brought these men here, who are [guilty of] neither temple robberies nor blasphemous speech about our goddess. **38 Now then, if Demetrius and his fellow tradesmen who are with him have a grievance against anyone, <u>the courts are open and proconsuls are [available]; let them bring charges against one another [legally]</u>**...40 For we are in danger of being called to render an account and of being accused of rioting because of [this commotion] today...41 And when he had said these things, he dismissed the assembly.*
>
> Acts 19:35-38, 40, 41 (AMPC)

So, who finally managed to silence this unruly riot when every previous attempt had failed miserably? Are you ready for this? It was a town clerk! The town clerk was an "officer of the court!" He released the authority of the court against this rioting mob. As a representative of the court, everybody recognized him and calmed down immediately. The town clerk then addressed Demetrius and his fellow tradesmen directly. He quickly established a legal procedure to settle the dispute between them and Paul. He said, "*the courts are open, and the pro counsels are available. Let them bring charges against one another legally.*" The clerk then dismissed the rioting mob, which minutes earlier was totally out of control, and they left quietly!

Idols Rioting on U.S Streets!

Recently, the United States of America went through something very similar to this story in the book of Acts. Peaceful protests over the unjust death of George Floyd, who died under police custody, were quickly overtaken by violent rioters. I believe these violent rioters were driven by their political idols and demonic belief systems (ideologies). Honest, hard-working business owners had their businesses looted, vandalized, and even burned to the ground as a result. Thankfully, the riot in Ephesus in Acts 19 gives us a model on how to silence "rioting idols" in our soul. *You must take them to the Courts of Heaven.* These heavenly courts are open 24/7 to hear any cases brought by God's children.

Getting this revelation was a game-changer for me. For years the idols in my life had been rioting. But I did not know how to silence them. Day and night, these demons worked tirelessly to drive me to chase after them. They simply never shut up! They were constantly speaking in my mind, telling me that to look and feel good, I needed to buy this product, or that gadget, or some new vitamin supplement, or the latest makeup line. They pushed me to cry out to my idols just like they drove the people of Ephesus into a riotous frenzy. No matter what I did, I couldn't get them to stop "rioting in my mind." That is until I got my soul healed and took these idols to the Courts of Heaven.

That is why Dr. Myles and I called this book "Idols Riot!" The spirits behind our idols have been terrorizing us for years! When these idols start "rioting" (driving you to do what they want), you lose your peace and mental clarity and become obsessed with fulfilling these idols' desires. If you have a shopping idol in your soul, it will send you on an out-of-control spending spree. You will find yourself charging things to your credit card you don't need. In the aftermath, you find yourself paying off your credit card bill for months to come. If your idol is eating, the demon behind it will drive you to the grocery store to buy more food than fits in your refrigerator. Or worse, those idols will take you on a daily drive to your favorite fast food joint.

Answer This!

Are you going through situations similar to what I am describing above? If so, then recognize that idols are rioting in your soul! They are crying, "You've got to have me to feel better! "If you buy this, you will be satisfied." "This product will vastly improve your life!" "You need this procedure because it is going to make you look younger!" These idols are shouting at you, trying to drive you to spend your time, energy, and money on them instead of trusting God to do something miraculous! Since demons never get tired, they won't ever shut up! You will only silence them by getting your soul healed then by taking them to court to revoke their legal rights.

Shut Up!

These demon-gods are continually going up to the Courts of Heaven, to present evidence of your adulterous involvement with them! They know that you have already broken the first commandment; *"You shall have no other gods before me!"* Consequently, you are "guilty as charged." The evidence they have gathered against you enables Satan to levy accusations against you in the Courts of Heaven. Once, the Lord showed me an evidence office in the second heaven. It was full of boxes and file cabinets stuffed with paperwork. I asked the Holy Spirit, "What's that?" He said, "That's the evidence Satan has accumulated every time you broke the laws of God." As I looked at the piles of paperwork, I knew this evidence included my sins of idolatry. I also knew that if I didn't show up for court, the enemy would keep winning "default judgments" against me. The same goes for you. The enemy has gathered not only massive evidence of your idolatry but also that of your ancestors! You need to go into court to face those charges so the blood can acquit you of Jesus, and the idols will be forced to shut up!

Taking the Strongman to Court

According to Isaiah 10:1-5, the Assyrian king accuses you of idolatry in the Courts of Heaven. This demonic principality is responsible for appointing corrupt judges who issue unrighteous decrees, and magistrates who cause unjust and oppressive decisions to be recorded in his court against children of God. Read what the passage says:

> *"Woe to those [judges] who issue unrighteous decrees, and to the magistrates who keep causing unjust and oppressive decisions to be recorded, 2 To turn aside the needy from justice*

*and to make plunder of the rightful claims of the poor of My
people, that widows may be their spoil, and that they may make
the fatherless their prey!...5 Woe to the Assyrian, the rod of My
anger, the staff in whose hand is My indignation and fury
[against Israel's disobedience]!*

Isaiah 10:1-5 (AMPC)

You need to turn the tables on the Assyrian king by taking *him* to
the Courts of Heaven. He has been issuing unrighteous decrees against
you that have caused you to be plundered of your rightful "claims," the
Bible says are yours. That is the reason many of your prayers aren't
answered. You have a legal right to everything that is in God's Word.
However, when you sin with idols, this enables this strongman to levy
charges against you in the Courts of Heaven, which then blocks the full
manifestation of your God-given promises. You must go to court to
reverse these unrighteous decrees that the Assyrian king has filed against
you. Don't forget that you must first bind the strongman before you can
thoroughly ransack his house. Remember, there are millions of idols in
the world, and the only way you have a chance to defeat them all is by
first taking out their "headship." You do this by getting your soul healed
of everything you have in common with this demonic strongman and
then by taking him to the Courts of Heaven.

Summon the Assyrian king to the Ancient of Days Court

One morning, I was led by the Lord to issue a subpoena to
summon the Assyrian king into the Courts of Heaven. Immediately, I
heard the Holy Spirit shout, "Watch out! Here comes the Ancient of
Days!" Then I saw a vision of the Assyrian king being brought into a

place called "The Ancient of Days Court." The prophet Daniel spoke of this heavenly court in the seventh chapter of the book of Daniel.

> *I kept looking until thrones were placed [for the assessors with the Judge], and the Ancient of Days [God, the eternal Father] took His seat, whose garment was white as snow and the hair of His head like pure wool. His throne was like the fiery flame; its wheels were burning fire. A stream of fire came forth from before Him; a thousand thousands ministered to Him and ten thousand times ten thousand rose up and stood before Him; the Judge was seated [the court was in session] and the books were opened."*

Daniel 7:9-10

What a powerful passage concerning the heavenly courtrooms! As I saw the Assyrian king being brought into this particular court, I realized this was the heavenly court where the *Ancient of Days,* God Himself, adjudicated. Consequently, this is the highest court in the heavens. Among other things, it is the place demonic strongmen are judged for Jesus to be given ultimate authority in the Universe!

> *And as for the rest of the beasts, their power of dominion was taken away; yet their lives were prolonged [for the duration of their lives was fixed] for a season and a time. 13 I saw in the night visions, and behold, on the clouds of the heavens came One like a Son of man, and He came to the Ancient of Days and was presented before Him. 14 And there was given Him [the Messiah] dominion and glory and kingdom, that all peoples, nations, and languages should serve Him. His dominion is an everlasting dominion which shall not pass away, and His kingdom is one*

which shall not be destroyed.

Daniel 7:12-14

Every evil strongman will eventually face judgment in the Ancient of Days Court so that Messiah can have total dominion over every person and nation. Your part in these ongoing court proceedings is to summon the Assyrian strongman into the Ancient of Days Court so he can be judged for his evil activity against God's people. As you enter into court, repenting over your idolatry, you will win your case against him; then, the Assyrian king will be bound and punished for his treasonous actions against you. Then you will be able to ransack the house of idolatrous demons that are under his control and stop their assaults against your life; thus, silencing their ability to drive you to pursue worthless idols. You will be free of their control.

At the end of each chapter, Dr. Myles and I created some powerful prayers that will help you prosecute and silence every idol and evil altar in the Courts of Heaven by first starting with a case against the Assyrian king in the Ancient of Days Court.

The Grace Court

Once you take the Assyrian king to the Ancient of Days Court, then you will be in the perfect position to ransack his house. Every idolatrous spirit under him can then be removed from controlling your life, including any spirit driving you to eat, spend money excessively. Every spirit striving to afflict your physical body, destroy your marriage, and even block your physical gifts will be stopped. The Bible says God commands every idolatrous spirit to come into His Courtroom to prove their divinity. That is a legal case they can never win because these idols are not God; they are demons.

"[You idols made by men's hands, prove your divinity!] Produce your cause [set forth your case], says the Lord. Bring forth your strong proofs, says the King of Jacob. Behold, you [idols] are nothing, and your work is nothing!"

Isaiah 44:9

Once the Ancient of Days Court releases a restraining order against the Assyrian king, you can then summon into court every other idol that is afflicting you and force them to prove their case against you. These cases are heard in the "Grace Court." In the world's judicial systems, there are many different categories of courts. A few examples are civil, criminal, and family courts, and in the United States, there is also the Supreme Court. Everything on earth is fashioned after the governmental pattern of heaven. Like the earth below, the spiritual realm has different courts of law. As you have seen, one of them is the Ancient of Days Court, but another is called the Grace Court. The writer of Hebrews declares, *Let us therefore come boldly to the throne of grace, that we may obtain mercy and find grace to help in time of need.* Hebrews 4:16, (NKJV)

The Greek word for throne in this verse is "thronos," which means a "seat" used by kings or judges that is "equivalent to [a] tribunal or bench." The throne in Hebrews 4 is not just a chair that God sits on; it is the bench from which the Judge of all the earth releases justice and mercy for His people through His glorious grace! The Grace Court is one of the most important courtrooms in Heaven when it comes to defeating idols. Why? The number one accusation Satan brings against you in the Courts of Heaven is your lawbreaking. The top two commandments of the Lord are: *"Thou shall have no idols before Me nor make for yourself any graven images."* Idolatry is the breaking of God's laws. Fortunately, according to scripture, grace is a power that can wipe out all your sins of lawbreaking, including you're idolatry. Look at this powerful example from scripture.

> *Then Law came in, [only] to expand and increase the trespass [making it more apparent and exciting opposition]. But where sin increased and abounded, grace (God's unmerited favor) has surpassed it and increased the more and super abounded. —*
>
> Romans 5:20

When the sin of your lawbreaking through your idolatry increases and abounds, God's grace will always surpass and superabound over your sin! That is an important truth to know. When you decide to destroy every idol in your life, Satan will fight back. He will try to tempt you and drive you into idolatry like never before. The demon gods behind your idols will come at you with all they have, and Satan will be there to accuse you in court every time you submit to their temptations and fall. So how do you protect yourself? The Lord, through the power of His grace, has made it possible for you to overcome all of the devil's indictments. The Apostle Paul explains how in this powerful verse.

> *I do not set aside and invalidate and frustrate and nullify the grace (unmerited favor) of God. For if justification (righteousness, acquittal from guilt) comes through [observing the ritual of] the Law, then Christ (the Messiah) died groundlessly and to no purpose and in vain. [His death was then wholly superfluous.]*
>
> Galatians 2:21AMPC

The Bible says it's impossible to keep the whole law (James 2:10). That's why Jesus, *the only sinless person in the history of the earth,* fulfilled the righteous requirements of the law for you on the cross

(Romans 8:4). Grace is the power that imparts this truth to you so that you can be justified, made righteous, and acquitted of every charge the enemy brings against you of your lawbreaking. That's why you must do as Paul said: never set aside, invalidate, frustrate, or nullify God's grace in your life. You need grace because it imparts Christ's righteousness to you. If you think you can walk perfectly before God without breaking His commandments, you are mistaken. Believing so would say that you didn't need Jesus to die for you and that He was crucified in vain!

As you continue to rely on the Lord to be your righteousness instead of your ability to keep the law, you will stand firm and protected against all accusations of the devil related to your idolatry.

Remember, no one can keep the law, which is why we need grace. Grace imparts Christ's righteousness to us so we can be acquitted of every accusation the devil brings against us of our idolatry. That's precisely what the verse below states.

> *We are justified (acquitted, declared righteous, and given a right standing with God) through faith. . . Through Him also we have [our] access (entrance, introduction) by faith into this grace (state of God's favor) in which we [firmly and safely] stand.*

> Romans 5:1–2 AMPC

The only way you can stand safely against the constant accusations of the enemy is if you *stay* in grace and repentance. Only then will you be totally justified before God and acquitted of every charge the devil brings against you. That is why the Grace Court is so important.

> *Let us then fearlessly and confidently and boldly draw near to the throne of grace (the throne of God's unmerited favor to us*

sinners), that we may receive mercy [for our failures] and find grace to help in good time for every need [appropriate help and well-timed help, coming just when we need it].

Hebrews 4:16 (AMPC)

Have you ever heard the expression "throw yourself on the mercy of the court?" That is what happens in this heavenly courtroom. In this court, all decisions and rulings of the judge are based on God's grace and mercy. The best news is that any believer can boldly enter this court to receive grace and mercy in their time of need, and when they do, they will receive *well-timed help, coming just when they need it.*

Before I share an amazing healing testimony that happened when I took someone into the Grace Court to get a judgment against an idolatrous spirit, I want to touch upon one more thing. Whenever you go

The Grace Court is one of the most important court-rooms in heaven when it comes to defeating idols.

into any court in heaven, you must posture yourself before the court through BOTH repentance and grace. It's never one or the other, as some teach. We need them both. Now that you know the importance of grace in defeating the enemy's accusations against your lawbreaking, I want you to understand that repentance is equally needful. Idolatry is sin, and sin always requires repentance. Many people say that because you are under grace, you don't need to repent anymore. I disagree completely. Look at how these verses connect repentance with the release of God's grace in your life.

Blessed [forgiven, refreshed by God's grace] are those who mourn [over their sins and repent], for they will be comforted [when the burden of sin is lifted].

Matthew 5:4, AMP

Blessed [forgiven, refreshed by God's grace] are you who weep now [over your sins and repent], for you will laugh [when the burden of sin is lifted].

Luke 6:21, AMP

Repentance is how you enter into the grace that is already yours! Notice that these verses say you are refreshed by God's grace *when you repent*. Think about it. The Bible says God gives grace to the humble. (1 Peter 5:5) There is no better way to humble yourself than to get on your knees and repent before God concerning your sins of idolatry. When you do, grace will be released to cover you with Christ's righteousness. Then you will be acquitted of your lawbreaking of idolatry. I could continue expounding on the importance of releasing *both* repentance and grace in the courts, but I will let Dr. Myles speak on them in the next chapter.

Testimony

I recently had an extraordinary victory over idolatrous spirits by taking them to the Courts of Heaven. As a result of winning the case, I saw an awe-inspiring miracle. I was in Minnesota doing a healing session. While praying for a young man, I heard the words "numbness in the toes." I asked the man if he was experiencing any numbness, but he was not. Then a woman named Sharie, who was sitting next to us, said that she did. When I asked her for details, she told me a horrible story.

Sharie had recently had knee-replacement surgery. She said that in completing the procedure, doctors misaligned her leg bone when they sewed her up. As a result, the tendons in her foot loosened when she walked, causing the bone to slip forward and protrude through her arch! You could actually see a bulge where the bone was jutting through her arch. Because of this, she could put no weight on her leg. She also had numbness and pain in her toes because the bone was pressing on a nerve and cutting off circulation in one of her arteries.

I immediately asked the Holy Spirit how I was to pray. That's when I heard Him say, "She has a tree growing in the middle of her leg." Instantly I knew what it meant. The Bible talks about the Israelites cutting down trees and carving statues out of them (Jer. 10:3; Isa. 44:14–15). Every person on this planet has some kind of idolatry in their life, and it appeared that Sharie was no exception. As a result, a spirit was blocking her healing. (Don't forget: the Bible says that idols cannot walk. Thus, I believe the spirits behinds these idols can cause crippling disorders!) With no time to explain, I told Sharie to repeat after me as I took her into the Grace Court, had her repent of her idolatry, then had her decree grace scriptures over herself.

Finally, I asked the Holy Spirit to heal her soul of any trauma she endured connected to her disorder. Then I asked the Holy Spirit to take away the numbness and pain. Finally, I rebuked the demonic spirit that was afflicting her. I commanded the bone to move, and it did! (I was just as shocked as she was!) She said, immediately all numbness and pain in her foot left, and she could put her weight on her foot and walk without hobbling. Suddenly, she also realized that the bulge in her arch was gone! A woman sitting next to her had seen the protrusion before the miracle happened. She also came up on stage to testify that it was no longer there! Sharie's arch looked perfect. Her healing was so complete that she told us she would cancel the surgery she had scheduled to reposition the bone.

The Power of Taking Idols to Court

Taking idols to court will dramatically change your life, and you will even experience healing miracles firsthand, as Sharrie did! A great example in the Bible is the man in Lystra. He was crippled in his feet from birth because of a wound in his soul. In that story, his miracle took place while everyone was standing near the city gate, the place where court decisions were executed. The Bible says this,

> And the crowds, when they saw what Paul had done, lifted up
> their voices, shouting in the Lycaonian language, The gods have
> come down to us in human form! [13] And the priest of Zeus, whose
> [temple] was at the entrance of the town, brought bulls and
> garlands to the [city's] gates and wanted to join the people in
> offering sacrifice. [14] But when the apostles Barnabas and Paul
> ...dashed out among the crowd, shouting, 15 Men....you should
> turn away from these foolish and vain things (Idols-Authors
> Emphasis) to the living God, Who made the heaven and the earth
> and the sea and everything that they contain."

Acts 14: (AMPC)

The gate of the city was the place where court was held. There were two altars on the trial docket that day: the evil altar of the demon god Zeus and the Godly altar inside Paul and Barnabus. Just as Dagon couldn't stand next to the Ark of the Covenant without ending up with his face in the dirt, neither could the enemy stand next to these godly servants of God. God won His case, and the crippled man was healed as Paul testified in court that the people should not follow "vain things" like idols.

Life Application Section

Memory Verse

Now then, if Demetrius and his fellow tradesmen who are with him have a grievance against anyone, the courts are open and proconsuls are [available]; let them bring charges against one another [legally].
Acts 19:38

Reflections

1. What is the best way to silence idols when they are rioting?

_____

_____

_____

_____

_____

2. Who stopped the crowd from rioting in Ephesus and why did the crowd listen to him?

_____

_____

_____

_____

_____

Prayer of Release #5

Summoning The Assyrian King Into The Courts Of Heaven

"Heavenly Father, I ask for the Court of Heaven to be seated, as I come before the Judge of all the earth to plead my case so I can be justified and proven right. I am here in court with my official representative, the Holy Spirit, my advocate and counselor. Heavenly Father, I surrender all rights to self-representation. Instead, I summon my defense attorney and mediator of the new covenant, the Lord Jesus Christ, to represent me in your Royal Courtroom. Heavenly Father, today I ask for permission to enter into the Ancient Days Court so I can prosecute an evil strongman who is opposing Jesus' reign on earth, the Kingdom of Heaven on earth, and everything pertaining to my life. I file a motion to summon, in the name of Jesus Christ, the Assyrian king who is the strongman over all idols, to the Ancient of Days Court to face criminal persecution. This strongman is responsible for issuing unrighteous decrees against all of God's blood-bought people. As it is written in Isaiah 10:1-2, *"Woe to those [judges] who issue unrighteous decrees, and to the magistrates who keep causing unjust and oppressive decisions to be recorded, ² To turn aside the needy from justice and to make plunder of the rightful claims of the poor of My people, that widows may be their spoil, and that they may make the fatherless their prey!"* It is also written in Isaiah 10:5, *Woe to the Assyrian, the rod of My anger, the staff in whose hand is My indignation and fury [against Israel's disobedience]!*

Now, LORD, these scriptures prove that the Assyrian king is causing unjust and oppressive decisions to be recorded in the Courts of

Heaven against Your people. The Bible also says the foundation of Your throne is justice and righteousness, so this gives us the lawful right to summon him to appear for prosecution in the Ancient of Days Court. I hereby summon the Assyrian king and other strongmen over idols (unknown to us but known to the Court). I do this per Mark 3:27, which says, *"But no one can go into a strong man's house and ransack his household goods right and left and seize them as plunder unless he first binds the strong man; then indeed he may [thoroughly] plunder his house."* I intend to seek a righteous verdict against him and all strongmen over idols so that I can thoroughly ransack every idolatrous spirit under him in his house.

My intention in this summons is to stop the idols from rioting in every area of my life. These idols are shouting nonstop in my mind and driving me mentally, physically, and emotionally to sin and pursue them. According to Acts 19:38, when the idols were rioting in Ephesus against Paul's message of the gospel, the city clerk, who was an officer of the court, said this to Demetrius and his tradesmen, *"Now then, if Demetrius and his fellow tradesmen who are with him have a grievance against anyone, the courts are open and proconsuls are [available]; let them bring charges against one another [legally]."* After the office of the court made that statement, the idols were silenced, and the riot stopped.

Heavenly Father, Righteous Judge, I now humbly ask for the Ancient of Days Court to be seated to adjudicate this case. I ask the books be opened, so that all the records of the accusations of my sins of idolatry and erecting evil altars that the Assyrian king has brought against me and my bloodline can be read aloud in court. I also ask my Books of Destiny be read aloud in Court, so that the will of the Lord can be done entirely in my life.

I now enter a plea of 'guilty' into the court's records concerning setting up idols and evil altars in my bloodline. The Bible says in Matthew 5:25, *Come to terms quickly [at the earliest opportunity] with your opponent at law while you are with him on the way [to court], so that your opponent does not hand you over to the judge, and the judge to the guard, and you are thrown into prison.* " Righteous Judge, since I am under oath, I cannot lie about my sinful activities and all transgressions connected to idolatry. I agree with any legitimate accusations brought against me and my ancestral bloodline by Satan and the Assyrian king. I submit a plea of guilty to all charges connected to any kind of idolatry that my ancestors or I ever committed. I now formally submit my guilty plea to the court in Jesus' Name. *And they overcame him by the blood of the Lamb and by the word of their testimony, and they did not love their lives to the death.* Revelation 12:11 (NKJV)

As I am called to testify on the witness stand, I humbly repent of all the charges leveled against me so I can overcome the enemy through the power of the blood and the word of my testimony. I repent of all sin connected to setting up idols and evil altars. I repent of lusting after them and allowing myself to be controlled by these evil altars. I repent for spending money on them and coming into partnership and fellowship with them. I repent for all sins that I have in common with any strongmen over idols. I put my sin under the blood of Jesus so I can overcome the enemy through my Redeemers' blood, in Jesus' Name.

Heavenly Father, Righteous Judge, now that you cleansed me by the blood of Jesus from every sin that I and my bloodline had in common with the Assyrian king and all strongmen over idols, I now move on the court to permanently bind the Assyrian king and issue a divine restraining order against him, and all demonic strongmen over idols, in

Jesus' Name. Lord, having secured this righteous verdict, I now seek the Court's permission to move into the Grace Court so that I can ransack the strongman's house.

I step boldly into the throne of Grace so that I can receive grace and mercy in my time of need according to Hebrews 4:16 which says, *"Let us then fearlessly and confidently and boldly draw near to the throne of grace (the throne of God's unmerited favor to us sinners), that we may receive mercy [for our failures] and find grace to help in good time for every need [appropriate help and well-timed help, coming just when we need it]."*

I now summon into this Grace Court every idolatrous demonic spirit under the Assyrian king or any other strongman over idols, so I can face the charges they have brought against me and get a righteous verdict against them. For it is written, *"You idols made by men's hands, prove your divinity!] Produce your cause [set forth your case], says the Lord. Bring forth your strong proofs, says the King of Jacob."* Because of the authority of this scripture, every demon spirit must respond to the summons and come into court now. I have already filed a guilty plea with heaven's court concerning my sins of idolatry and the erecting of evil altars. I now throw myself on the mercy of this court, that I can receive grace and mercy in my time of need.

Heavenly Father, Righteous Judge, I decree that because of the blood of Jesus and the power of His grace, my bloodline and I must be acquitted of all charges of idolatry, as well as the sin of erecting evil altars. Heavenly Father, as I continue to testify in this court, I also decree that I am under the power of the free and unmerited Grace of God. Since the Bible says it's impossible to keep the whole law, I need grace. I admit to this court that my sins of idolatry, bowing to evil altars, and spending my money on these evil altars have increased and abounded. But now, I decree Grace has increased even the more over my sin and even superabounded. I also decree these following grace verses over myself so that the enemy's charges will have to be dismissed.

[Therefore, I do not treat God's gracious gift as something of minor importance and defeat its very purpose]; I do not set aside and invalidate and frustrate and nullify   the   grace (unmerited favor) of God. For if justification (righteousness, acquittal from guilt) comes through [observing the ritual of] the Law, then Christ (the Messiah) died groundlessly and to no purpose and in vain. [His death was then wholly superfluous.]

Galatians 2:21

For while the Law was given through Moses, grace ([a]unearned, undeserved favor and spiritual blessing) and truth came through Jesus Christ.

John 1:17

But if you are guided (led) by the [Holy] Spirit, you are not subject to the Law.

Galatians 5:18

For sin shall not [any longer] exert dominion over you, since now you are not under Law [as slaves], but under grace [as subjects of God's favor and mercy].

Romans 6:14

Now, Invite Jesus To Heal Your Soul!

Holy Spirit, I now invite you to search my soul (my will, mind, and emotions) and judge and heal the wound in my soul connected to evil strongmen. The word strongmen means to have the strength of soul to resist the attacks of Satan. I believe, LORD, you are strengthening my soul against the strongman now by your blood and the action of the Holy Spirit. Lord Jesus, I am asking You to cleanse my soul with your blood, to cleanse my soul of every sin of idolatry, and to cleanse my soul of every evil altar that has been erected in my inner man. The Bible says it's the blood that atones for the soul. The Bible also declares that the blood cleanses my conscience; thus, I decree the blood is cleansing my mind right now of all thoughts connected to idolatry. I decree the blood is cleansing my will so that any demon strongman won't control it. I declare the blood is also cleansing my emotions to sever them from the control of idols and evil altars. Lord Jesus, I am asking You to also pour out the anointing of "Dunamis Power" to heal every wound in my soul that is in common with the Assyrian king. As it is written in Isaiah 10:27; *"And it shall be in that day that the burden of [the Assyrian] shall depart from your shoulders, and his yoke from your neck. The yoke shall be destroyed because of fatness [which prevents it from going around your neck].*

Finally, I decree and declare that I am full of the light of Christ and that my body and my will, mind, and emotions are healed of everything that is in common with the Assyrian king. As written in Isaiah 10:17-18 *And the Light of Israel shall become a fire and His Holy One a flame, and it will [a]burn and devour [the Assyrian's] thorns and briers in one day. 18 [The Lord] will consume the glory of the [Assyrian's] forest and of his fruitful field, both soul and body; and it shall be as when a sick man pines away or a standard-bearer faints.*

I decree the truth of this verse over myself right now. The light of Christ is becoming a fire, and it will burn away all the briers and thorns of the Assyrian in my body and soul IN JUST ONE DAY!!!!!!!!

Loudly Declare These Supernatural Decrees So You Can Have Your Breakthrough!

Heavenly Father

- I decree and declare that the Assyrian king and the strongmen are bound, and I am ransacking their house.

- I decree and declare that all legal claims stolen from me by the Assyrian king are now restored to me, in Jesus' Name.

- I decree that every unrighteous, unjust, oppressive decrees and decisions he has recorded against me are now broken and overturned right now.

- I decree and declare that all rightful claims that belonged to me are being released right now.

- I decree and declare that the Grace Court has given me special grace to prevail against all idols and evil altars that were under the strongman's control in Jesus' Name.

- I decree and declare that the idols must now stop rioting and driving me to sin in Jesus' Name.

- I decree and declare that every idol and evil altar ever erected in my bloodline is destroyed by the blood and grace of Jesus Christ in Jesus' Name.

- I decree and declare that the Lord Jesus has judged the Strongman, Assyrian king, and every idol that submits to this demonic principality, in Jesus' Name. Amen.

Time to Take Communion

Lord, as I take this communion, I do it in remembrance of You and Your victory on the cross and the resurrection. I decree that as I drink this cup of Your blood and eat Your body, my sins are forgiven, and my soul is nourished and refreshed and strengthened. I decree that as I eat Your flesh and drink Your blood, I will never be hungry and thirsty for idols again. I decree that as I partake of Your supper that my "Not Guilty" verdict from this Court concerning "setting up evil altars in my life and bloodline," will be sealed by the power and testimony of Your body and blood in Jesus' Name

THE IDOLS ARE RIOTING

6

Prosecuting Evil Altars in the Courts of Heaven

by

Dr. Francis Myles

That night the Lord said to Gideon, Take your father's bull, the second bull seven years old, and pull down the altar of Baal that your father has and cut down the Asherah [symbol of the goddess Asherah] that is beside it; [26] *And build an altar to the Lord your God on top of this stronghold with stones laid in proper order. Then take the second bull and offer a burnt sacrifice with the wood of the Asherah which you shall cut down.* [27] *Then Gideon took ten men of his servants and did as the Lord had told him, but because he was too afraid of his father's household and the men of the city to do it by day, he did it by night.* [28] *And when the men of the city arose early in the morning, behold, the altar of Baal was cast down, and the Asherah was cut down that was beside it, and the second bull was offered on the altar which had been built.* [29] *And they said to one another, Who has done this thing? And when they searched and asked, they were told, Gideon son of Joash has done this thing.* [30] *Then the men of the city commanded Joash, Bring out your son, that he may die, for he has pulled down the altar of Baal and cut down the Asherah beside it.* [31] *But Joash said to all who stood against him, Will you contend for Baal? Or will you save him? He who will contend for Baal, let him be put to death while it is still morning. If Baal is a god, let him contend for himself because one has pulled down his altar.* [32] *Therefore on that day he called Gideon Jerubbaal, meaning, Let Baal contend against him, because he had pulled down his altar.*

Judges 6:25-32

ৡৢৡৢ

THE ABOVE PASSAGE of scripture gives us a prophetic template on the importance of bringing down, destroying, and prosecuting the evil altars of our father's house or bloodline. Gideon had just finished having a face-to-face encounter with God. One would think that this would be enough to release Gideon into his God-given destiny fully. However, the Angel of the Lord appeared to Gideon a second time to bring judgment from the Courts of Heaven against the altar of Baal that was in his father's house. Please remember that in scripture, anytime you see "judgments or sentences" being passed on things, places, people, or demonic entities, the judgments are coming directly from the Courts of Heaven. Judgments require judicial activity to be set in motion. The Lord gave Gideon very specific instructions on how to bring down the evil altar of his father's house. Then the Lord told him to build an altar to the Lord at the exact same spot his father had used to build an altar to Baal or the goddess Asherah.

First, it is interesting to note the language the angel of the Lord used when he told Gideon to go and destroy the altar of his father's house. The Lord said, *"build an altar to the Lord your God on top of this stronghold."* This statement's implied principle is obvious: the evil altar Gideon's father had built to his idol was the biggest stronghold over Gideon's family. Perhaps this is why the Lord did not allow Gideon to move into his destiny until the idol's stronghold and its altar in his bloodline were destroyed. The moral of the story is that if we don't overthrow idols in our souls and bloodline and the evil altars that they rule from, it will be difficult for us to live a life of sustained break-through.

Secondly, we see that when Gideon went to destroy the evil altar of his father's house, he went at night and took ten of his servants. These servants helped Gideon fulfill God's instruction to destroy the evil altars of his father's house. There is a redemptive principle in the story that we can follow. It is simply this: some idols in our lives we cannot pull down by ourselves without being accountable to a group of brothers and sisters who share the same spiritual goal. Thankfully, Gideon, even though he was afraid, faithfully executed the judgment of God against the evil altar of his father's house. When he followed through, there was an immediate breakthrough in his family, and his destiny as a judge in Israel was released.

Thirdly the angel of the Lord told Gideon to sanctify the new altar to the Lord with a sacrificial offering. That is an important part of the whole process of prosecuting and bringing down evil altars. Listen to what the great King David has to say about this in Psalms 96:8, *"Give to the LORD the glory due His name; Bring an offering, and come into His courts."* All altars are raised and sustained by the sacrifices of their human attendants. Thus, you need to have an offering that is speaking for you in the Courts of Heaven against the idols and evil altars you want to see destroyed in your life. King David shows us in the above scripture that one of the ways we give God the glory due His name is to come into His courtroom with an offering.

I am convinced that the reason the angel of the Lord wanted Gideon to destroy the evil altar of his father's house is that it was being used by Satan in the Courts of Heaven to level endless accusations against Gideon and his family. Had Gideon tried to move into his destiny without prosecuting the evil altar of his father's house, Satan would have retained the legal right to deny his destiny from manifesting in the earth. This is why this chapter on prosecuting evil altars from the Courts of Heaven is very important.

Without a shadow of a doubt, the most challenging fight you will ever face with idols and evil altars is when the LORD sends you to tear down the evil altar of your father's house and to dethrone the idol that sits on it! Be warned! Why? Because the idols and evil altars of your father's house were planted in the family bloodline by your forefathers. They, for the most part, were men or women in positions of authority over the family. Deceived by the devil, they willingly opened the door to the family bloodline to the idol(s) and the evil altar(s) that are now firmly planted in your generational lineage.

Knowing this truth, I now have some very good news for you: evil altars, no matter their spiritual classification, can be prosecuted in the Courts of Heaven. Just like the United States of America has a Department of Justice (a well-organized judicial system), God's Kingdom has the most robust judicial system in the universe. Most importantly, the Courts of Heaven are the highest Court of Appeals available to mankind. It is far-reaching in its jurisprudence and jurisdiction. By definition, the word "prosecute" means to "institute legal proceedings against (a person) or an entity in a court of law." I have already stated that altars are living entities and the idols that sit on them are actually demonic personalities. By law, both can be prosecuted in the Courts of Heaven.

Nothing in Common

I will not talk with you much more, for the prince (evil genius, ruler) of the world is coming. And he has no claim on Me. [He has nothing in common with Me; there is nothing in Me that belongs to him, and he has no power over Me.]

John 14:30

The first thing we must do before prosecuting any evil altar in the Courts of Heaven is to make sure that we have nothing in common with the evil altar we want to prosecute. If we have anything in common with the evil altar or if our soul enjoys some of the pleasurable attributes the altar brings, then when we try to prosecute Satan, he will retain the legal right to resist receiving an action from the Courts of Heaven.

Jesus is the one who taught us the power of this principle. He triumphantly declares in the above passage that the prince of this world, the evil genius ruler of this present darkness, was coming after Him. Thankfully Jesus said Satan had no legal "claim" on Him. Interestingly enough, Jesus used the word "claim" in describing Satan's approach because the word "claim" is a legal term. By law, the word means "to assert and demand the recognition of (a right, title, possession, etc.)" Jesus knew that Satan was about to put him on trial on the Cross of Calvary to see if He was qualified to be the Savior of the world and the appropriation for our sin. If Jesus had sin in his life, Satan would have every legal right to drag the soul of Jesus to hell and deny Him the miracle of the resurrection. Thankfully for all of us, Jesus had nothing in common with Satan and his kingdom of darkness. There was no darkness or shadow of turning in Christ! This condition of holiness gave Jesus the most powerful position of stature in the Courts of Heaven. That is why the following step is essential if we want to successfully prosecute evil altars in our lives.

Repent!

If we [freely] admit that we have sinned and confess our sins, He is faithful and just (true to His own nature and promises) and will forgive our sins [dismiss our lawlessness] and [continuously] cleanse us from all unrighteousness [everything not in conformity to His will in purpose, thought, and action].

1 John 1:9

Before we enter the Courts of Heaven to prosecute evil altars, we must first examine ourselves and repent of any areas of sin the Lord reveals to us. Especially sins that are connected to the evil altar we are trying to prosecute. In God's Kingdom, one of the most important things we can ever do is "repent." To "repent" means to *"change one's mind and go in a different direction."* The above passage of scripture makes it clear that God is more than willing to forgive us of our sin and cleanse us from any unrighteousness if we simply repent of it. *Repentance restores and secures our spiritual stature in the Courts of Heaven.* Most importantly, repentance removes every legal right that Satan is holding against us in the Courts of Heaven.

Evil altars, no matter their spiritual classification, can be prosecuted in the Courts of Heaven

We cannot afford to allow Satan to provide legal evidence against us in the Courts of Heaven that would prove that we are actually in love with some of the fruits of the evil altar we are trying to destroy. That is why I have a problem with proponents of the grace message who teach that we don't need to repent after we come to Christ because we are not under the law but under grace. This type of demonic teaching is precisely what Satan ordered because he knows the importance of repentance in winning cases in the Courts of Heaven. Rest assured, the devil doesn't want you to repent! He wants you to use the grace of God as a cloak of unrighteousness (1 Peter 2:16)! However, notice the above verse states that when we repent, God will *forgive our sins and dismiss our lawlessness!* Please remember that the first and second commandments of God confront the sin of idolatry head-on. *Repentance is a vital part of getting Satan's accusations of our idolatrous lawbreaking dismissed in court!*

Court is in Session

I kept looking until thrones were placed [for the assessors with the Judge], and the Ancient of Days [God, the eternal Father] took His seat, Whose garment was white as snow and the hair of His head like pure wool. His throne was like the fiery flame; its wheels were burning fire. [10] *A stream of fire came forth from before Him; a thousand thousands ministered to Him and ten thousand times ten thousand rose up and stood before Him; the Judge was seated [the court was in session] and the books were opened.*

Daniel 7:9-10

Once we have repented of what the Lord showed us, we need to come before the Courts of Heaven in a spirit of boldness, knowing that the Lord, our righteous judge, longs to hear our voice in His Courtroom. In the above passage of scripture, the prophet Daniel shows us the Court of Heaven's seating and decorum. Daniel saw thrones being put in place, including the throne of the Ancient of Days. The thrones in this particular text are thrones of judgment and justice. The seats in this prophetic vision are judicial seats.

Interestingly enough, the Bible says, "*the Judge was seated [the court was in session] and the books were opened.*" That is very similar to what happens in the courts of men here on earth. If you have ever attended a trial in a courtroom, you probably noticed that the court is never considered to be "in session" until the judge is seated and the evidence (Books) presented.

One of the first things that I do when I come before the Courts of Heaven to prosecute cases against demonic powers is to ask the Court to be seated. I ask the Court of Heaven to be seated to adjudicate my case in Jesus' Name. Then I ask for the evidence books to be opened as I present my case in faith, knowing that "if we do anything according to His will, the Bible says He hears us," and we will have the thing we petitioned.

Come Before the Grace Court

Let us therefore come boldly to the throne of grace, that we may obtain mercy and find grace to help in time of need.

Hebrews 4:16 (NKJV)

Prosecuting Evil Altars in the Courts of Heaven

My dear friend Katie Souza did an excellent job in the previous chapter explaining the importance of bringing our idols and prosecuting them in the Grace Court. Since all idols demand that an altar is built for them by their human attendants, it's impossible to separate idols from altars. They are inseparable. You can't have one without the other, since altars provide demonic spirits with legal entry into the world of men. The evil altars upon which our idols sit must also be summoned to appear in the Grace Court. Without the grace of God, we can do nothing of eternal consequence.

> *For it is by grace [God's remarkable compassion and favor drawing you to Christ] that you have been saved [actually delivered from judgment and given eternal life] through faith. And this [salvation] is not of yourselves [not through your own effort], but it is the [undeserved, gracious] gift of God."*

Ephesians 2:8

I want you to meditate on the far-reaching spiritual implications of the scripture above. It says grace is God's remarkable compassion and favor that draws us to Christ. That is why you want to take the idols and the evil altars in your life to the Grace Court because it is filled with God's remarkable compassion and favor for you and me.

Secondly, the passage also tells us that it is by *grace through faith* that we have been *delivered from judgment*! Remember what I mentioned earlier? The word "judgment" speaks of judicial activity in a courtroom. So, it's grace that saves us from judgment in the Courts of Heaven. Since Satan is a legalist and uses the law to terrorize us, when we come into the Grace Court, we nullify his ability to use the law against us, making it easy to prosecute both idols and evil altars in the Courts of Heaven.

The Prosecution of an Evil Altar

And behold, there came a man of God out of Judah by the word of the Lord to Bethel. Jeroboam stood by the altar to burn incense. [2] The man cried against the altar by the word of the Lord, O altar, altar, thus says the Lord: Behold, a son shall be born to the house of David, Josiah by name; and on you shall he offer the priests of the high places who burn incense on you, and men's bones shall be burned on you. [3] And he gave a sign the same day, saying, "This is the sign which the Lord has spoken: Behold, the altar shall be split and the ashes that are upon it shall be poured out."

1 Kings 13:1-3

The above passage of scripture shows us a biblical case study of an actual prosecution of an evil altar in the Courts of Heaven. The trial of this evil altar started with a nameless man of God sent by the Word of the Lord to Bethel. Why Bethel? There was an evil national altar that the devil was using to contaminate the people of Israel spiritually and control the nation's destiny. This grieved the God of Israel, who had chosen Israel's people to be a holy nation unto Himself. When the man of God arrived in Bethel, he discovered to his dismay that King Jeroboam was the human attendant to this evil altar. The man of God proceeded with the prosecution of this altar by speaking directly to the altar itself. At first, he completely ignored the presence of the king at the

Without the grace of God we can do nothing of eternal consequence.

evil altar. He proceeded to pronounce the prescribed judgment of God against the evil altar. In other words, the prophet of God, *who was acting as an officer of the Court of Heaven, publicly read God's righteous verdict against the evil altar.*

The Signs of a Judged Evil Altar

When King Jeroboam heard the words the man of God cried against the altar in Bethel, he thrust out his hand, saying, Lay hold on him! And his hand which he put forth against him dried up, so that he could not draw it to him again. ⁵ The altar also was split, and the ashes poured out from the altar according to the sign which the man of God had given by the word of the Lord. ⁶ And the king said to the man of God, "Entreat now the favor of the Lord your God and pray for me, that my hand may be restored to me." And the man of God entreated the Lord, and the king's hand was restored and became as it was before.

1 Kings 13:4-6

So, what are the tell-tale signs that God has judged an evil altar in the Courts of Heaven? How do we know that the Court has removed its power? These are crucial questions. Thankfully, we have a solid biblical example to guide us in knowing when an evil altar has been judged. In the above passage of scripture, when King Jeroboam heard the words of the man of God, which he spoke against the evil altar, he was furious. He tried to have the man of God arrested but failed. Instead, the hand he tried to use to strike the man of God withered instantly. Terrified, he begged the man of God to entreat the LORD to heal his hand. The man of God prayed to the Lord and asked Him to heal the king's hand. Immediately, the king's hand was restored as before. Soon after, the evil altar was also split into pieces. The ashes on the altar poured out, falling helplessly to the ground!

The Holy Spirit showed me several tell-tale signs of when an evil altar is under divine judgment from the Courts of Heaven. I will quickly list these signs for you.

1. The human attendant to the evil altar loses the power or ability to influence or control others using the evil altar's voice. That means that God silenced the voice of the evil altar. He made it mute and dumb in the spirit world as He did with the altar of Baal on Mount Carmel (1 Kings 18) when the 400 prophets of Baal cut themselves with knives hoping their sacrifice would make Baal speak on their behalf, but they were gravely disappointed.

2. Supernatural power shifts from the evil altar to the man of God. When an evil altar is judged, it's influence, power, and oppression over the person or family are broken permanently, and an increase of anointing, power, and authority takes its place.

3. God's power splits the evil altar into pieces, making future use by anyone impossible. That means that once an evil altar has been prosecuted and judged in the Courts of Heaven, its malicious activities in the believer's life or family unit stops. I believe the exact opposite will begin to take place. For instance, if God judges an altar of poverty, then financial prosperity will start to flow freely in the lives of people who were previously bound by an evil altar of poverty.

4. The power of sickness and witchcraft are completely broken. God's healing power is released to heal people previously infected by the

evil altar. I believe that many of the people reading this book are going to be healed and delivered when the evil altar that held them captive is prosecuted and destroyed in the Courts of Heaven.

5. God turns yesterday's ashes into something beautiful when the ashes from the altar fall to the ground. That is a prophetic picture of how God will restore the spiritual, emotional, and financial fortunes of people previously bound by the evil altar.

Close the Door & Throw Away the Key

And the king said to the man of God, "Come home with me and refresh yourself, and I will give you a reward. [8] *And the man of God said to the king, if you give me half your house, I will not go in with you, and I will not eat bread or drink water in this place.* [9] *For I was commanded by the word of the Lord, You shall eat no bread or drink water or return by the way you came.* [10] *So he went another way and did not return by the way that he came to Bethel.*

1 Kings 13:7-10

In closing, one of the most important things we must do once an evil altar has been prosecuted and judged in the Courts of Heaven *is to close the door and throw away the key!* What do I mean by this? The devil and demons hate to lose anybody. Remember, demons are hunters of the priceless souls of men. These malicious spirits are desperate for legal access to the world of men. Demons know that once they are cast out of a person or family bloodline, they lose their legal authority to function in the earth realm. So, Satan will always try to see if he can re-erect the evil altar in the bloodline of the person who has just been delivered by the power of God. In other words, *Satan is not going to leave without attempting to return.* In the above passage of scripture, when King Jeroboam realized that the evil altar from which he drew his power had been destroyed, he tried to befriend and bribe the prophet of God. In other words, he tried to see if he could create something in common between the man of God and the evil altar that had just been destroyed. As a messenger of Satan, the king was trying to reopen a portal for a demonic return.

Refuse to Compromise!

Thankfully the man of God refused to compromise his godly standards. He was not going to touch or defile himself with anything connected to the evil altar that used to be in Bethel. Jesus already told us what happens in the spirit world when an unclean spirit is cast out of a man. Listen to what Jesus said:

> *But when the unclean spirit has gone out of a man, it roams through dry [arid] places in search of rest, but it does not find any.* [44]*Then it says, I will go back to my house from which I came out. And when it arrives, it finds the place unoccupied, swept, put in order, and decorated.* [45] *Then it goes and brings with it seven other spirits more wicked than itself, and they go in and make their home there. And the last condition of that man becomes worse than the first. So, also shall it be with this wicked generation.*
>
> Matthew 12:43-45

Jesus is telling us that whenever we cast out a demon or any demonic entity, the "spirit or thing" will look for ways to return to its original place of occupation if the "person delivered" is careless or foolish enough to re-open the door to the demonic. *I pray that you will not do that! Your time of limitless breakthrough has come!*

Life Application Section

Memory Verse

When King Jeroboam heard the words the man of God cried against the altar in Bethel, he thrust out his hand, saying, Lay hold on him! And his hand which he put forth against him dried up, so that he could not draw it to him again. ⁵ The altar also was split, and the ashes poured out from the altar according to the sign which the man of God had given by the word of the Lord. ⁶ And the king said to the man of God, "Entreat now the favor of the Lord your God and pray for me, that my hand may be restored to me." And the man of God entreated the Lord, and the king's hand was restored and became as it was before. 1 Kings 13:4-6

Reflections

1. What was King Jeroboam's relationship with the evil altar at Bethel?

_____

_____

_____

_____

2. How can you prosecute an evil altar in the Courts of Heaven?

_____

_____

_____

_____

_____

Prayer of Release #6

Prosecuting Evil Altars

"Heavenly Father, I ask for the Court of Heaven to be seated, as I come before the Judge of all the earth to plead my case so I can be justified and delivered from the evil altars of my father's house. I am here in court with my official representative, the Holy Spirit, my advocate and counselor. Heavenly Father, I surrender all rights to self-representation; instead, I summon my defense attorney and mediator of the New Covenant, the Lord Jesus Christ, to represent me in your Royal Courtroom. Heavenly Father, I am in your Supreme Court to prosecute all idols and evil altars controlling my life and bloodline, in Jesus' Name. Heavenly Father, Satan can no longer retain any legal rights to deny my destiny from manifesting in the earth.

I now enter a plea of 'guilty' into the court's records concerning setting up evil altars in my bloodline. The Bible says in Matthew 5:25, *Come to terms quickly [at the earliest opportunity] with your opponent at law while you are with him on the way [to court], so that your opponent does not hand you over to the judge, and the judge to the guard, and you are thrown into prison."* Righteous Judge, since I am under oath, I cannot lie about my sinful activities and transgressions connected to my idolatry. I agree with any legitimate accusations brought against me and my ancestral bloodline by Satan. I submit a plea of guilty to all of Satan's charges connected to any kind of idolatry that my ancestors or I committed. I now formally submit my guilty plea to the court in Jesus' Name. Amen. *And they overcame him by the blood of the Lamb and by the word of their testimony, and they did not love their lives to the death.* Revelation 12:11 (NKJV)

As I am called to testify on the witness stand, I humbly repent of all the charges leveled against me so that I can overcome the enemy through the power of the blood and the word of my testimony. So, I repent of all sin connected to setting up evil altars. I repent on behalf of my forefathers who established these evil altars. I will not allow myself to be controlled by these evil altars. I repent for spending money on them and coming into partnership and fellowship with them. I repent for anyone in my bloodline who set up altars to gods of harvest, fertility gods and goddesses, and to Molech, the god of child sacrifice, I repent for setting up altars to stars and constellations, the sun and the moon, and I also repent for setting up altars to marine spirits and gods of war. I repent for setting up altars to any Egyptian gods or goddesses. I repent for setting up altars to music gods and goddesses. I repent for setting up altars to the gods of witchcraft and magic. I repent for setting up altars to the gods and goddesses of death. I repent for setting up altars to the gods and goddesses behind occultic knowledge and wisdom. I repent for setting up altars to the gods and goddesses behind Halloween. I repent for setting up altars to the gods and goddesses behind sexual perversion. I plead with the court to put my sin under the blood of Jesus so I can overcome the accuser through my redeemers' blood. In Jesus' Name.

As I continue to testify in this court, I also decree that I am under the power of the free and unmerited Grace of God. Since the Bible says it's impossible to keep the whole law, I need the grace of the Lord Jesus Christ. I admit to this court that my sins of idolatry, bowing to evil altars, and spending my money on these evil altars, have increased and abounded. But now I decree Grace has increased over my sin and even super abounded. I also decree Psalms 118:27 over myself.

The LORD is God, and He has given us light [illuminating us with His grace and freedom and joy]. Bind the festival sacrifices with cords to the horns of the altar.

Heavenly Father, Righteous Judge, I decree that because of the blood of Jesus and the power of His grace, my bloodline and I must be acquitted of all charges of erecting evil altars in our lineage. Heavenly Father, I request that You go back to the first time my ancestors erected these evil altars to their lifeless idols and judge these evil altars. Righteous Judge, I ask you to use your judicial discretion to reverse every generational curse over my life." In Jesus' Name. Amen.

Now, Invite Jesus To Heal Your Soul!

Holy Spirit, I now invite you to search my soul (my will, mind, and emotions) and judge every idol and evil altar in my life and bloodline. I surrender every soul wound to you, Lord, for it's You who leads me beside the still waters and restores my soul. Lord Jesus, I am asking You to cleanse my soul with your blood, to cleanse my soul of every sin of idolatry, and to cleanse my soul of every evil altar that has been erected in my inner man. The Bible says it's the blood that atones for the soul. The Bible also declares that the blood cleanses my conscience; thus, I decree the blood is cleansing my mind right now of all thoughts connected to idolatry. I decree the blood is cleansing my will so that evil altars won't control it. I declare the blood is also cleansing my emotions to sever them from the control of idols and evil altars.

Lord Jesus, I am asking You to also use your "Dunamis Power" according to Acts 10:38 to heal every wound in my soul that any evil altar uses to control me, oppress me, attack me, and speak to me. I also decree Ephesians 3:16 over myself that my soul is being strengthened and re-enforced by mighty Dunamis Power through the Holy Spirit. Thus, I am being strengthened in my soul to resist the control of these bloodline altars. They won't be directing my thoughts, my emotions, or my will anymore. Finally, I decree and declare that I am full of the light of Christ. Psalm 118 says that God has given us his light, which will illuminate our soul with his grace, freedom, and joy in Jesus' Name. Amen.

Loudly Declare These Supernatural Decrees So You Can Have Your Breakthrough!

Heavenly Father

- I decree and declare that since the evil altar to the gods of the harvest is destroyed, I will reap in business, in investments, in my retirement accounts, bank accounts, and projects.

- I decree and declare that now, since the evil altar to the gods of fertility is destroyed, my body will be fertile, including all of my reproductive organs, in Jesus' Name.

- I decree and declare that now, since the evil altar to Molech, the god of child sacrifice, is destroyed, I will never again experience abortion, in my physical body, in my businesses, in my investments, in my retirement accounts, in my bank accounts, or any of my projects

- I decree and declare that now since the evil altar to the sun, moon, and stars, and the altars to the gods of war are destroyed, I decree and declare that I will not be afraid of the terror of the night nor of the arrow that flies by day. I decree and declare that I will not be struck by the pestilence that stalks in darkness, nor of the destruction (sudden death) that lays waste at noon. The Lord is my keeper, and as Psalms 121 says, He shall preserve my soul and heal my body.

- I decree and declare that since the evil altars to marine spirits and the gods and goddesses behind sexual perversion are destroyed, I have total victory over all sexual sin and all demonically induced sexual dreams and nightmares.

- I decree and declare that since the evil altar to music gods and goddesses is destroyed, I will no longer have an appetite or be driven to listen to worldly music, which does not edify my soul.

- I decree and declare that since the evil altar to the gods of witchcraft and magic is destroyed, I will never operate in a spirit of witchcraft or manipulation or be the victim of anyone operating in these spirits

- I decree and declare that since the evil altars to the gods and goddesses of death are destroyed, my flesh will become fresher than a child's, my youth will be supernaturally renewed. I will not die before my appointed time.

Time to Take Communion

Lord, as I take this communion, I do it in remembrance of You and Your victory on the cross and the resurrection. I decree that as I drink this cup of Your blood and eat Your body, my sins are forgiven, and my soul is nourished and refreshed and strengthened. I decree that as I eat Your flesh and drink Your blood, I will never be hungry and thirsty for idols again. I decree that as I partake of Your supper that my "Not Guilty" verdict from this Court concerning "setting up evil altars in my life and bloodline," will be sealed by the power and testimony of Your body and blood in Jesus' Name.

THE IDOLS ARE RIOTING

7
Losing Your Money to Idols

by

Katie Souza

But as time went on, there arose no little disturbance concerning the Way [of the Lord]. 24 For a man named Demetrius, a silversmith, who made silver shrines of [the goddess] Artemis [Diana], brought no small income to his craftsmen. 25 These he called together, along with the workmen of similar trades, and said, Men, you are acquainted with the facts and understand that from this business we derive our wealth and livelihood.

Acts 19:23-25 AMPC

৽৽৽

THE BIBLE SAYS in John 10:10, the devil comes to *steal, kill, and destroy.* One of his most effective ways to decimate your life is to cause you to spend money on idols. The proof of this is in the story of the riot that happened in Ephesus. Demetrius, the man who sparked this city-wide uprising, bragged that he "brought no small income" from his business of selling useless shrines of the goddess Artemins. He was so good at hawking lifeless statues to suckers that he made "big bucks" doing it. Demetrius even stated that he and his fellow craftsmen derived their "wealth and livelihood" from their selling lifeless idols.

These peddlers were getting rich off selling useless pieces of metal to the gullible public. How sickening is that? Yet the same thing is happening all over the world today. Though many upright businesses

---

161

offer quality products that solve real-life problems, there are also many more who sell nothing more than empty promises. Ultimately, it is the buyer (you) that decides whether or not they succeed.

How many silver "trinkets" have you either sold to an unsuspecting buyer or purchased to find satisfaction and emotional fulfillment? Maybe you went through a dozen or more products before you found the one that delivered the results you wanted. Are you one of those people who has bottles of unwanted shampoos, conditioners, soaps, oils, lotions, and face creams under your sink? Do you have racks of clothing and shoes that never get worn, even though you had to have it when you saw those items in the store? I know of people who lost everything due to a gambling addiction or because they tried to compete with the "Joneses" next door! Whatever the case, the idols we chase generate a lot of money for the merchants that sell them. These modern-day silversmiths derive their wealth from us as we continue to spend wads of cash on securing the latest thing our soul is lusting after. It's clear, if we don't get healed of the idols in our soul, we will continue to bleed money. God wants to release your finances from the control of these worthless idols because the more you spend on them, the more you create a landing strip for them to steal from you, make you sick, devastate your marriage, and destroy your businesses. Not to mention that the more money we waste on our soulish idols, the less money we will have to fund the gospel of Jesus Christ!

The Assyrian King Robs People & Nations

For [the Assyrian king] has said, I have removed the boundaries of the peoples and have robbed their treasures; [14] *And my hand has found like a nest the wealth of the people;*

and as one gathers eggs that are forsaken, so I have gathered all the earth; and there was none that moved its wing, or that opened its mouth or chirped.

Isaiah 10:13-14

In the above passage, the Assyrian king boasts about how he robs people and nations of their treasures. In the ancient world, Assyria went from kingdom to kingdom, forcefully confiscating their wealth and resources. Unfortunately, he is doing the same thing today when we give him the legal right to do so. What does the Assyrian king's statement, "I have removed the boundaries of the peoples," actually mean? The word "boundaries" is an expression that represents "the discipline of divine restraint." The Assyrian king is a demonic principality who uses the idols in your soul to drive you to break free of the divine restraints God provides to resist temptation. You see, idolatry causes you to lose control over your impulses. This spirit brings temptation in front of you, then moves in for the kill. The next thing you know, you have whipped out your credit card to pay for your latest soul desire. This is one of the many ways the Assyria king *"removes your God-given boundaries and robs you of your treasures (money)."*

In the above scripture, the Assyrian king also claims that he has the power to steal your "nest eggs." Isaiah 10:14 says, *"And my hand has found like a nest the wealth of the people;'* What does this mean? He dips his hand into your savings account, retirement funds, investments, stock, and bonds and gathers them to himself. He accomplishes this by driving you to make decisions based on greed, which leads you to pursue ventures that go upside down and bring significant financial loss. He also accomplishes this *fleecing of your nest egg* by getting you to recklessly spend your savings on investments that never pan out or increase in value. If a nation and its people are embroiled in the sins of idolatry, such as the case in America, this strongman spirit can influence the country's financial systems to cause an economic recession that results in financial losses in your 401k or retirement accounts.

King Hezekiah Gives God's Money to the Assyrian King

One of the many kingdoms Assyria robbed was Jerusalem. Shalmaneser, king of Assyria, besieged neighboring Samaria. He took her people captive and then set his eyes on the City of David. Eventually, Jerusalem was surrounded by about 185,000 bloodthirsty Assyrian soldiers. They were threatening to put the people under a famine so severe that they would be forced to drink their urine and eat their feces. Hezekiah was king over Jerusalem at the time. Before the siege, he had already been on a campaign to cleanse the city of its idolatry, which is what positioned Jerusalem to receive one of the most astounding supernatural deliverances chronicled in the Bible. Overnight, an angel slew all 185,000 Assyrian soldiers while the Israelites slept safely in their beds. Let's look closely at this incredible story so you can walk in the same spiritual authority once you are cleansed of your idolatry.

> *In the third year of Hoshea son of Elah king of Israel, Hezekiah son of Ahaz king of Judah began to reign.* [3] *Hezekiah did right in the sight of the Lord, according to all that David his [forefather] had done.* 4 *He removed the high places, broke the images, cut down the Asherim, and broke in pieces the bronze serpent that Moses had made, for until then the Israelites had burned incense to it; but he called it Nehushtan [a bronze trifle]...* [7] *And the Lord*

was with Hezekiah; he prospered wherever he went. And he rebelled against the king of Assyria and refused to serve him.

2 Kings 18:1, 3-4, 7 AMPC

Hezekiah started his righteous reign doing what God is calling all His people to do today, break to pieces every idol that has taken possession of their life. Hezekiah was so driven to eradicate all idolatry that he even rebelled against the strongman over every idol, *the Assyrian king*, by refusing to serve him. However, shortly after Hezekiah's cleansing campaign, the Assyrian king rose and took the fortified cities surrounding Jerusalem. That frightened Hezekiah and diminished his resolve to continue resisting the invasion. Hezekiah finally caved to the pressure from the Assyrian king. Like all sophisticated street-thugs, the Assyrian then took him for everything he had.

Then Hezekiah king of Judah sent to the king of Assyria at Lachish, saying, I have done wrong. Depart from me; what you put on me I will bear. And the king of Assyria exacted of Hezekiah king of Judah 300 talents of silver and thirty talents of gold. [15] And Hezekiah gave him all the silver that was found in the house of the Lord and in the treasuries of the king's house. [16] Then Hezekiah stripped off the gold from the doors of the temple of the Lord and from the doorposts which he as king of Judah had overlaid and gave it to the king of Assyria.

2 Kings 18:14-16

Hezekiah was a very godly king. Nevertheless, when the Assyrian king put the screws to him, he folded by giving the extortioner money! The Assyrian king was living up to his claim of robbing the nations of their treasures and stealing their nest eggs. The worst part was that Hezekiah didn't just turn over his personal finances, but he also gave him all the silver in the Lord's temple. He even went as far as stripping the gold from the doors of the temple!

It's horrible to think that Hezekiah would rob the house of God to give those riches to the king who is over every idol. But how many times have we done the same thing? Instead of bringing our whole tithe into the storehouse, we spent it on our idols. Members of a church or ministry partners driven by the idols in their soul rob God of the tithes and offerings due His glorious name! Then they are cursed

If a nation and its people are embroiled in the sins of idolatry, the strongman can influence the country's financial systems to cause an economic recession

with a curse, as the Book of Malachi states. *That is why we must get healed of these idols and dismantle their evil altars in our life.*

Why would Hezekiah do something as reckless as rob the temple and give its resources to the strongman over idols? Especially after he had cleansed Jerusalem of all its ungodly altars and vowed never to serve the Assyrians? He obviously had something in his soul that was "in-common" with that demon god, so it had control over him. I believe the legal landing strip in Hezekiah's life was not only from ancestral idolatry but also from an evil altar that his father erected in his bloodline.

Altars in your Bloodline Drive you to Submit to Idols

Hezekiah's father, King Ahaz, was an idol worshipper. The Bible says he made molten images of the god Baal. He even burnt his sons in the fire as an offering to his evil gods. He sacrificed to idols in the "high places." Ahaz was such an idolater that he gave financial tribute to, you guessed it, the strongman over all idols, the king of Assyria!

And Ahaz took the silver and gold in the house of the Lord and in the treasuries of the king's house and sent a present to the king of Assyria.

2 Kings 16 AMPC

Take note that King Ahaz committed the same sin his son Hezekiah would later repeat. King Ahaz and Hezekiah both stripped the temple of its silver and gold and gave it to the Assyrian king! How ironic. This is how generational iniquities get their foothold in our lives. Someone in your bloodline opens the door to idolatry. Then the demons they worshipped continue to steal from their descendants, driving them to spend money on idols, even if they have to take that money from the house of God!

When someone in your bloodline opens the door to idolatry, you will end up displaying the same sinful behavior generations later, just as Hezekiah repeated his father's sins. That is why we need to destroy the idols and evil altars in our souls that came from the sins in our bloodline. We must take these evil altars and the demon gods behind them to court. If we don't, we will keep repeating our ancestors' sins, and their idols will keep plundering our treasures and stealing our nest eggs.

Destroying Ungodly Altars that Steal Your Money

Again, Hezekiah was a very godly king who was totally against idolatry. We see this clearly when he cleansed Jerusalem of all its unholy statues, obelisks, and high places. Nevertheless, he still did something as shocking as robbing the temple of God. Yet this was to be expected, as he was just following in his father's footsteps. King Ahaz not only soldout to the devil by robbing the temple and giving the money to the Assyrian king, but he also built an unholy altar in Jerusalem. As you will see, he sacrificed his wealth to Assyrian gods on this unholy altar! Look at the details of this sordid story:

> *King Ahaz went to Damascus to meet Tiglath-pileser king of Assyria and saw their [heathen] altar. King Ahaz sent to Urijah the priest a model of the altar and an exact pattern for its construction. [11]So Urijah the priest built an altar according to all that King Ahaz had sent from Damascus, finishing it before King Ahaz returned. [12]When the king came from Damascus, he looked at the altar and offered on it. [13]King Ahaz burned his burnt offering and his cereal offering, poured his drink offering, and dashed the blood of his peace offerings upon that altar.][14]The bronze altar which was before the Lord he removed from the front of the house, from between his [new] altar and the house of the Lord and put it on the north side of his altar. [15]And King Ahaz commanded Urijah the priest: Upon the principal (the new) altar, burn the morning burnt offering, the evening cereal offering, the king's burnt sacrifice and his cereal offering, with the burnt offering and cereal offering and drink offering of all the people of the land; and dash upon the [new] altar all the blood of the burnt offerings and the sacrifices. But the [old] bronze altar shall be kept for me to use to inquire by [of the Lord].*

> 2 Kings 16:10-15 AMPC

Inside the temple in Jerusalem, King Ahaz built a replica of the evil altar the Assyrians had erected in the city of Damascus! Then he kept sacrificing on it every day! King Ahaz became the human attendant to this evil altar, which meant his physical body gave the demonic spirits connected to that altar the legal right to operate in Jerusalem. His sinful actions also allowed the devil to plant this evil altar in his bloodline, passing its influence down to his son Hezekiah.

Notice how the above passage of scripture says that Ahaz made that altar from Assyria *the principal altar*. In other words, he officially designated this demonic altar as being the first in importance. He gave all his sacrifices to it. That is one of the biggest reasons why his godly son Hezekiah could not resist robbing the temple to give the money to the Assyrian king. Let us recall what Dr. Myles said in an earlier chapter: *"The altar of the Lord demands offerings, such as blood, peace offerings, first-fruits, tithes, alms, and so forth. Since the devil is a master copycat, his evil altars also demand sacrifice from the human attendant who has allowed these demon-gods to build altars in their soul or bloodline."*

King Ahaz had built an altar dedicated to the demon king, who rules over all idols. He gave unholy sacrifices on that altar. As a result, its demonic influence was passed down through his bloodline. *It eventually ended up controlling Hezekiah's actions!* The presence of this evil altar in Hezekiah's bloodline caused him to hand over substantial financial reserves to a demonic power. That is why we must cleanse our bloodline of every evil altar established by our ancestors. If we don't, the demons behind these altars will continuously direct the way we spend our money, in addition to robbing our nest eggs and plundering our treasures. Later on in this book, Dr. Francis Myles has a powerful testimony on how the Holy Spirit helped him demolish an evil altar erected by his forefathers. When he demolished the evil altar, he experienced life-changing and explosive financial breakthroughs!

Please note what King Ahaz said in the above verse about the altar of God, which was in the temple when he brought in the evil altar from Assyria. *"But the [old] bronze altar shall be kept for me to use to inquire by [of the Lord]."* Ahaz was content to sacrifice to his idols while still having a relationship with God! In essence, he kept the Lord's altar around so he could get information and guidance from God while continuing to sacrifice to his idols. That sounds so much like the Body of Christ today. We spend our money, energy, and time on our selfish desires and demon idols while still asking God to stick around so He can guide us into success, freedom, deliverance, and healing.

Fortunately, Hezekiah finally overcame the evil influence his father's altar possessed over his life, which led to a massive victory over the Assyrians. It also resulted in Hezekiah having personal wealth beyond imagination! How did he do it? Believe it or not, it was through giving a massive and sacrificial offering.

Take an Offering into the Court

There is always a biblical solution or antidote to whatever ails you. First and foremost, to break the chokehold the Assyrian king has over your finances, you must come before the Courts of Heaven with a "special and sacrificial peace offering." You cannot come empty-handed before the Judge of all the earth. If you do, you are breaking the spiritual protocol established by God in Psalms 96:8, *"Give to the Lord the glory due His name; bring an offering and come [before Him] into His courts."*

You are told to come into the courts of the LORD to "give Him the glory due His name." How do you accomplish this critical task? According to the last part of the verse, "by bringing an offering into His courts." This makes a lot of sense because Satan already has legal accusations against you in the Courts of Heaven for spending God's money on the idols in your soul or bloodline. So how do you break Satan's legal accusations on your money plus demonstrate your renewed allegiance to God's Kingdom? You bring a special and sacrificial offering into the Courts of Heaven. This offering will then begin to speak for you in the Court each time Satan or the Assyrian king brings up an accusation against your finances. If you take a closer look at Psalm 96, you will see how it connects bringing an offering with defeating every idolatrous spirit.

> *For great is the Lord and greatly to be praised; He is to be reverently feared and worshiped above all [so-called] gods.* [5] *For all the gods of the nations are [lifeless] idols, but the Lord made the heavens.* [6] *Honor and majesty are before Him; strength and beauty are in His sanctuary...* [8] *Give to the Lord the glory due His name; bring an offering and come [before Him] into His courts.*

> Psalms 96:4-6,8 AMPC

There is no coincidence that this Psalm calls for you to bringing an offering in His courts *after* it calls the so-called gods and idols of this world *lifeless*. The *power of your seed brought into heaven's courts* will *put to death every strategy these gods have devised to destroy you.* Just look at the proof in Hezekiah's story.

Hezekiah's Offering Destroys the Assyrian king

After Hezekiah removed all the idols in Jerusalem, the Bible says He then took a massive offering to the Lord. First, Hezekiah brought into the temple his personal contributions. Then he commanded his people to give the portions due to the priests and Levites. The Bible shows how the people responded to the word from the King:

> *As soon as the command went abroad, the Israelites gave in abundance the firstfruits of grain, vintage fruit, oil, honey, and of all the produce of the field; and they brought in abundantly the tithe of everything. 6 The people of Israel and Judah who lived in Judah's cities also brought the tithe of cattle and sheep and of the dedicated things which were consecrated to the Lord their God, and they laid them in heaps. 7 In the third month [at the end of wheat harvest] they began to lay the foundation or beginning of the heaps and finished them in the seventh month.*

> 2 Chronicles 31:5-7 AMPC

Wow, a powerful spirit of giving to the LORD broke out after Hezekiah cleansed the land of idols. There was an unprecedented financial breakthrough the children of Israel had not seen for a very long time. Heaps and heaps of money came into the temple. That is how the high priest Azariah described what followed after the dismantling of idols and the giving of the offering, *"we have eaten and have plenty left, for the Lord has blessed His people, and what is left is this great store."* The Bible says that God blessed his people so much that there was still a great store leftover even after they had eaten. In fact, verse 11 says the overflow was so great that Hezekiah had to order the priests to build storage rooms to contain all the blessings!

Hezekiah and the people were not only repaid for everything that was stolen from the temple and given to the Assyrian king, but they were also paid back multiplied amounts over what they initially lost. That is what will happen to believers worldwide as we agree as one man to say NO to our idols. All the years of financial losses and destruction will be replenished! God will bring a 1000-fold return on everything we spent on idols, and revival will hit the nations like a ball of fire. In Hezekiah's story, the offering changed the economic status of the nation. Plus, as you will see, the Lord also used that same offering as a weapon to destroy the Assyrian army that surrounded Jerusalem! Let me prove it to you!

The Offering Cleanses Your Bloodline

Hezekiah had done all he knew to do. He removed idolatry from the land of Israel and brought a massive tithe into the courts of the Lord. Now, he was waiting for God to move. It was a scary moment. During the siege, Hezekiah had taken ill and was given the word by the prophet Isaiah that he was going to die. When the people of the city looked over their walls, they were confronted with the site of countless Assyrian soldiers waiting for their surrender. Food and water were running low. The situation could not have been worse. But God had a plan!

When Hezekiah turned his face to the wall and wept, the Lord gave another prophetic word to the prophet Isaiah. This is what He told him:

> *"Go and tell Hezekiah, 'Thus says the Lord, the God of David your father: "I have heard your prayer, I have seen your tears; surely I will add to your days fifteen years. I will deliver you and this city from the hand of the king of Assyria, and I will defend this city."*

2 Kings 20:5

Glorious light broke through the darkness of despair, and hope was immediately instilled into Hezekiah's heart. He was going to be healed, and Jerusalem would be delivered from the Assyrian's grip. Then the prophet Isaiah went on to tell the king what the sign would be that these things would happen.

> *"And this is the sign to you from the Lord, that the Lord will do this thing which He has spoken: 8 Behold, I will bring the shadow on the sundial, which has gone down with the sun on the sundial of Ahaz, ten degrees backward." So, the sun returned ten degrees on the dial by which it had gone down."*
>
> 2 Kings 20:7-8

This is the biggest recorded miracle in the entire Bible. Why? Because the sun doesn't move. For sunlight to turn back, the rotation of the planets would have to screech to a halt then start spinning backward! I find it super exciting that God would execute a cosmic level miracle *because his people were fighting the strongman over all idols*! That's how important this battle against idolatry is! ***Idolatry is the world's number one problem!*** That's why God will literally move the universe to free us from its iron grip!

Please take note that the sunlight turned back on the sundial of Ahaz. Why is this important? Every single detail of the Bible holds enormous significance. A *sundial is an ancient timekeeper*. There were many sundials in Jerusalem at that time. However, God made a point of explicitly saying the sunlight would go backward on the sundial that Hezekiah's father, Ahaz, had built. By this, the Lord was letting Hezekiah know that He was going back in time to cleanse his bloodline of all idolatry brought about by his father. God was wiping out that moment when Ahaz robbed the temple and then gave the money to the Assyrian king. The Lord was also removing the effects of the unholy altar Ahaz had erected to his Assyrian gods.

That is how the Lord rids you of everything in your bloodline that is "in-common" with these idols. He is the Alpha and Omega, the Beginning and the End, and the First and the Last. Through His Holy Spirit, He releases "Dunamis power" to heal every wound that came upon your soul because of the sins of your ancestors. Then our heavenly Father turns back time to completely cleanse your bloodline of every evil altar that was erected by your forefathers.

Shockingly, your tithe is a huge part of stepping into that miracle realm! The offering Hezekiah gave was key to the cosmic level miracle taking place in His life. How so? The Bible says the sunlight went back "10" steps on Ahaz's sundial. The word "ten" here comes from the Hebrew root word "asar," which means "to give a tithe!" Thus, the offering, given by Hezekiah and the people, opened the heavens so that time could go backward to wipe out all idolatry in their lives! Please recall what Malachi 3 says,

> *Bring all the tithes (the whole tenth of your income) into the storehouse, that there may be food in My house, and prove Me now by it, says the Lord of hosts, if I will not open the windows of heaven for you and pour you out a blessing, that there shall not be room enough to receive it. 11 And I will rebuke the devourer ... for your sakes and he shall not destroy the fruits of your ground."*
>
> Malachi 3:10-11

Yes, the massive heaps of finances Hezekiah and the people of Israel gave literally opened the windows of heaven, caused time to go back to the root of everything they had in-common with Assyria, and the devourer was rebuked! Shortly after, a warring Angel showed up in the middle of the night while everyone was sleeping. He killed every single

Assyrian soldier who was threatening the lives and economic security of the people of Jerusalem. The enemy lay dead in their tents, and the king of Assyria was driven back to his own country, where his sons killed him. How is that for poetic justice?

Financial Breakthrough Follows the Death of Idols

Even though this was the most spectacular display of power God had ever exhibited, He wasn't done yet. Hezekiah had endeared himself to the Lord by cleansing Jerusalem from idols and bringing in a massive tithe to the house of the Lord. Consequently, he became rich.

> *And Hezekiah had very great wealth and honor, and he made for himself treasuries for silver, gold, precious stones, spices, shields, and all kinds of attractive vessels, 28 Storehouses also for the increase of grain, vintage fruits, and oil, and stalls for all kinds of cattle, and sheepfolds. 29 Moreover, he provided for himself cities and flocks and herds in abundance, for God had given him very great possessions.*
>
> 2 Chronicles 32:27-29

The moral of this story is clear. If we get rid of idols in our soul and bring a peace offering into His heavenly courtroom, God will overthrow the Assyrian king, break his chokehold on our finances, and vastly increase our prosperity.

Bringing an Offering to Court causes a Wealth explosion

> *Give to the Lord the glory due His name; bring an offering and come [before Him] into His courts.*

Psalm 96:8

Please don't forget that King Hezekiah and the people of Israel didn't just give an ordinary tithe; they brought in an abundance of their first fruits!

> *As soon as the command went abroad, the Israelites gave in abundance the firstfruits of grain, vintage fruit, oil, honey, and of all the produce of the field; and they brought in abundantly the tithe of everything. ...6 and they laid them in heaps. 7 In the third month [at the end of wheat harvest] they began to lay the foundation or beginning of the heaps and finished them in the seventh month.*

2 Chronicles 32:5-7

They gave profusely of ALL the produce of the field. And they didn't just give once; they continued giving for the next four months until there were heaps in the temple! This opened the heavens and caused time to go back to everything in their bloodline that was allowing the Assyrian king to assault them. As you bring your BEST offering into the court, you will see the same result. Expect it! Time will turn backward on your Aunt Jessica or Uncle Steve to wipe out every idolatrous altar they erected that is now stealing your money!

Life Application Section

Memory Verse

And Hezekiah gave him all the silver that was found in the house of the Lord and in the treasuries of the king's house. 16 Then Hezekiah stripped off the gold from the doors of the temple of the Lord and from the doorposts which he as king of Judah had overlaid, and gave it to the king of Assyria. 2 Kings 18:15-16

Reflections

1. What did King Hezekiah do to the idols that were in Jerusalem?

_____

_____

_____

_____

_____

2. Why is it important to enter the courtroom with a sacrificial offering?

_____

_____

_____

_____

_____

_____

Prayer of Release #7

Prosecuting Money Stealing Idols

"Heavenly Father, I ask for the Court of Heaven to be seated, as I come before the Judge of all the earth to plead my case so I can be justified and delivered from the evil altars of my father's house. I am here in court with my official representative, the Holy Spirit, my advocate, and my counselor. Heavenly Father, I surrender all rights to self-representation; instead, I summon my defense attorney and mediator of the New Covenant, the Lord Jesus Christ, to represent me in Your Royal Courtroom. Heavenly Father, I am in Your Supreme Court to prosecute all idols and evil altars controlling my life and bloodline, in Jesus' Name. Heavenly Father, Satan can no longer retain any legal rights to deny my destiny from manifesting in the earth.

I now enter a plea of 'guilty' into the court's records concerning setting up evil altars in my bloodline. The Bible says in Matthew 5:25, *Come to terms quickly [at the earliest opportunity] with your opponent at law while you are with him on the way [to court], so that your opponent does not hand you over to the judge, and the judge to the guard, and you are thrown into prison."*

Righteous Judge, since I am under oath, I cannot lie about my sinful activities and transgressions connected to my idolatry. I agree with any legitimate accusations brought against me and my ancestral bloodline by Satan. I submit a plea of guilty to all of Satan's charges connected to any idolatry that my ancestors or I committed. I now formally submit my guilty plea to the court in Jesus' Name. *And they overcame him by the blood of the Lamb and by the word of their testimony, and they did not love their lives to the death.* Revelation 12:11 (NKJV)

As I am being called to testify on the witness stand, I humbly repent of all the charges leveled against me so that I can overcome the enemy through the power of the blood and the word of my testimony. I repent of all sin connected to financial idols and evil altars. I repent for acting like Demetrius by selling useless, powerless, silver shrines in the form of ineffective products and demonic business deals. I repent for buying useless silver shrines of demon gods, falling for getting-rich quick scams. I repent for doing what Kings Hezekiah and King Ahaz did, stealing money from the temple of the Lord to give to idols. I repent for doing what King Ahaz did when he built a replica of the unholy Assyrian altar and then brought all of his sacrifices to it. I repent for making all evil, money stealing altars the primary altars where I brought all my financial sacrifices, instead of bringing all of my offerings to the altar of the Lord. I repent anytime that I did not give God the glory due His name by bringing an offering into His courts. I announce my intention to bring a sacrificial, firstfruit offering at the end of this just as King Hezekiah and the people of Jerusalem did, right before they completely defeated the Assyrian king.

As I continue to testify in this court, I also decree that I am under the power of the free and unmerited Grace of God. Since the Bible says it's impossible to keep the whole law, I need grace. I admit to this court that my sins of idolatry and spending my money on idols have increased and abounded, but now I decree Grace has increased even the more over my sin and even super abounded. I also decree Romans 3:20 and 24 over myself.

For no person will be justified (made righteous, acquitted, and judged acceptable) in His sight by observing the works prescribed by the Law. [All] are justified and made upright and in right standing with God, freely and gratuitously by His grace (His unmerited favor and mercy), through the redemption which is [provided] in Christ Jesus,

Heavenly Father, by the blood of Jesus and the power of His grace, I must be acquitted of all charges of idolatry. I announce that I will be bringing my sacrificial offering into this courtroom like Hezekiah and the people of Jerusalem. And when I present my offering in this court, I am asking the court to use its supreme powers to bend back the curvature of time and space. I am asking that You cause the sun to move back 10 degrees on the sundial of my ancestors to wipe out every time they sinned by stealing finances from the Lord's temple by not bringing all the tithes and offerings into the house of the Lord, and when they built evil money altars. Heavenly Father, I request that You go back to the first time my ancestors erected an evil altar to their idols and then judge that altar to reverse this generational curse." In Jesus' Name, Amen

Now, Invite Jesus To Heal Your Soul!

Holy Spirit, I now invite you to search my soul (my will, mind, and emotions) and judge and heal every wound that came from the sins of not bringing the whole tithe into the house, by stealing money from the temple of the Lord, and from erecting an evil money altar that is in common with Assyria. The Bible says in 3 John 2 that *I will prosper even as my soul prospers.* So, Lord Jesus, I am asking You to cleanse my soul with Your blood, so that every wound in my soul connected to my finances can be cleansed. The Bible says it's the blood that atones for the soul. The Bible also declares that the blood cleanses my conscience; thus, I decree the blood is cleansing my mind right now of all thoughts connected to money that would shipwreck my finances. I decree the blood is cleansing my will so that it won't be controlled by evil, money stealing altars that drive me to make bad decisions with my finances. I declare the blood is also cleansing my emotions to sever them from the control of idols and evil altars that drive me to make emotional purchases.

Lord Jesus, I am asking You to also use Your "Dunamis Power," according to Acts 10:38, to heal every wound in my soul that any evil, money stealing altar is using to rob me, put poverty on me, and to attack me financially. I also decree Ephesians 3:16 over myself that my soul is being strengthened and re-enforced by mighty Dunamis Power through the Holy Spirit. Thus, I am being strengthened in my soul to resist not bringing in the whole tithe, taking my tithe money and spending it io idols, and spending my money lavishly and recklessly. These money stealing altars will not direct my thoughts, emotions, or my will anymore. Finally, I decree and declare that I am full of the light of Christ. As John 8:12 says, *"Once more, Jesus addressed the crowd. He said, "I am the Light of the world. He who follows Me will not walk in the darkness but will have the Light of life."* I decree my soul is not walking in darkness, and I have the light, which is life, so my finances will also be full of life.

Loudly Declare These Supernatural Decrees So You Can Have Your Breakthrough!

Heavenly Father

I decree and declare that the Assyrian king's influence is broken over my life so he can no longer rob my treasures and steal my nest eggs.

- I decree and declare that when I bring my sacrificial offering into the Courts of Heaven that You will turn back time on the sundial of my ancestors. Thus every Assyrian soldier that has me surrounded will be taken out by the angel of the Lord and that you will rebuke the devourer, and I will be free of all the famine and lack that held me captive.

- I decree and declare that I will now have the same explosive financial increase that Hezekiah had as written in 2 Chronicles 32:27-29! *Now Hezekiah had immense wealth and honor; and he made for himself treasuries for silver, gold, precious stones, spices, shields, and all kinds of delightful articles, [28] and storehouses for the produce of grain, new wine, and [olive] oil, and stalls for all kinds of cattle, and sheepfolds for the flocks. [29] Moreover, he made cities for himself and acquired an abundance of flocks and herds, for God gave him very many possessions.*

Time to Take Communion

Lord, as I take this communion, I do it in remembrance of You and Your victory on the cross and the resurrection. I decree that as I drink this cup of Your blood and eat Your body, my sins are forgiven, and my soul is nourished and refreshed and strengthened. I decree that as I eat Your flesh and drink Your blood, I will never be hungry and thirsty for idols again. I decree that as I partake of Your supper that my "Not Guilty" verdict from this Court concerning "setting up evil altars in my life and bloodline," will be sealed by the power and testimony of Your body and blood in Jesus' Name

THE IDOLS ARE RIOTING

8

Overthrowing Money Altars in Your Bloodline

by

Dr. Francis Myles

And the [threshing] floors shall be full of grain and the vats shall overflow with juice [of the grape] and oil. ^{25} *And I will restore or replace for you the years that the locust has eaten—the hopping locust, the stripping locust, and the crawling locust, My great army which I sent among you.* ^{26} *And you shall eat in plenty and be satisfied and praise the name of the Lord, your God, Who has dealt wondrously with you. And My people shall never be put to shame.*

Joel 2:24-26

ॐॐॐ

FINANCES ARE CRUCIAL to advancing God's Kingdom through His children here on earth. The church's primary assignment is to be fishers of men (souls). While the Messiah-Jesus is God's priceless gift unto all mankind, taking that gospel to the ends of the earth is very expensive. The Body of Christ needs a lot of money to fulfill its assignment! Unfortunately, one of the most critical and adverse effects of having idols in our soul is how they drive us to spend God's money on worthless things. In earlier chapters, we showed you that all idols (demon-gods) demand that an altar is built for them. Again, an altar is a place of sacrifice and exchange. So, these idols require that in exchange for the comfort they give us, we have to spend money on them. It's a fact - we spend a lot of money on our idols so that our souls can find some temporal comfort.

Be reminded of what the Bible says,

"Demetrius, a silversmith, who made silver shrines of [the goddess] Artemis [Diana?] It said he brought no small income to his craftsmen., When he called together, along with the workmen of similar trades, He said out of his own mouth, Men, you are acquainted with the facts and understand that from this business we derive our wealth and livelihood."

Acts 19:24

It's abundantly clear from the above passage that idolatry is a monetized demonic practice. Idolatry is monetized at both ends of the line:

1. Firstly, modern-day "Demetriuses" who create products that are idolized by others derive great wealth from selling these idols.
2. Secondly, consumers of idols spend vast amounts of money every year on their idols to comfort their idolatrous soul. In so doing, they create evil altars in their life that are serviced by all the "products" these idols drive them to buy!

These are just a couple of reasons why this chapter on overthrowing money altars is very important for us to understand. The reason most well-meaning Christians cannot seem to get ahead financially is that their bloodline is full of evil money altars. When there is an evil money altar in your bloodline, it gives the devil the legal right to demand that the altar is constantly serviced through financial sacrifices. Unfortunately, the human attendants in the bloodline that has been compromised by the idolatrous iniquity of their forefathers are the one that pays the bill. That is why some of you can't stop the impulse buying that causes you to purchase things you don't need. You have an evil altar in your bloodline that is driving you to spend, spend, spend.

Idols and Evil Altars are Everywhere!

In the twelfth year of Ahaz king of Judah, Hoshea son of Elah began his nine-year reign in Samaria over Israel. [2] *He did evil in the sight of the Lord, but not as Israel's kings before him did...* [12] *And they served idols, of which the Lord had said to them, You shall not do this thing.*

2 Kings 17:1-2,12

Many God-loving people may be tempted to say, "I have no idols or evil altars in my soul!" Well, guess what: this chapter is for you. While I honestly doubt there are any true followers of Jesus (*maybe a rare few*) who can truthfully say they have no idols in their life, it is crucial to understand another aspect of prosecuting idols and evil altars in the Courts of Heaven. *Every believer on earth has idols and evil altars that were established in their ancestral bloodline by their forefathers long before they accepted Messiah-Jesus as their personal Lord and Savior.* So now ask yourself, who is going to prosecute these idols and evil altars before the Courts of Heaven for the pain and destruction they have caused for many generations in your family bloodline?"

Please remember God raises and anoints deliverers for each family lineage on earth. I got saved in 1989 in the nation of Zambia.

Within a couple of years after that, every member of my immediate family of 11 were all gloriously born-again! God told me, "Francis, I have raised you as a deliverer to your family." I continue to play this critical role in my family. Maybe that's why you picked up this book. You are the "Moses" of your family, anointed by God to carry your bloodline to the promised land of destiny! That is why it falls on your shoulders to prosecute family idols and evil altars before the Courts of Heaven! You must destroy the evil money altars in your bloodline that are bleeding you and your family of much-needed finances!

Evil Money Altars in Job's Life

There was a man in the land of Uz whose name was Job; and that man was blameless and upright, and one who feared God [with reverence] and abstained from and turned away from evil [because he honored God]. ² Seven sons and three daughters were born to him. ³ He also possessed 7,000 sheep, 3,000 camels, 500 yoke (pairs) of oxen, 500 female donkeys, and a very great number of servants, so that this man was the greatest [and wealthiest and most respected] of all the men of the east (northern Arabia).

Job 1:1-3 (AMP)

The above passage of scripture is the first mention of a man by the name of Job. He was from the land of Uz. Biblical scholars all agree the book of Job is the oldest book in the Bible written before Moses wrote the Pentateuch, which are the first five books of the Bible. For the most part, Job is introduced as a God-fearing man who hated evil. In addition to this, scripture goes out of its way to state that Job was also very wealthy. In fact, the Bible says he was the richest man in the East. Needless to say, how did such a man lose all of his magnificent wealth in a very short time? Thankfully, when we allow the Holy Spirit to give us revelation, we discover things that were right in front of us that we could not see at first.

> *Now there was a day when the sons of God (angels) came to present themselves before the [d]Lord, and Satan (adversary, accuser) also came among them. [7] The Lord said to Satan, "From where have you come?" Then Satan answered the Lord, "From roaming around on the earth and from walking aroundon it." [8] The Lord saidto Satan, "Have you considered and reflected on My servant Job? For there is none like him on the earth, a blameless and upright man, one who fears God [with reverence] and abstains from and turns away from evil [because he honors God]."*

> Job 1:6-8 (AMP*)*

The above scripture begins to unravel the mystery of what happened to Job. The Bible brings us into a heavenly courtroom scene where Satan appears with a company of guardian angels who were returning from their earthly assignments. Before the Lord gave me the revelation about *operating in the Courts of Heaven,* this passage of scripture gave me serious challenges, theologically speaking. I said to myself, "Why is Satan in heaven when the Bible is clear that he was cast out of Heaven with 1/3 of the angels who rebelled against God?" Not long after this, the Lord showed me that *Satan is an officer of the Court of Heaven because no self-respecting judge would allow a trial to proceed without a prosecutor!*

The Holy Spirit showed me that even though Satan had been cast out of heaven, he still has been given limited access to the Courts of Heaven because he is the accuser of the brethren. No accusation can hold judicial weight unless it is presented in court, which is why Satan is still allowed in the heavenly courts. Suddenly, his presence in heaven in the book of Job made sense. Satan was there to bring accusations against the deeds of Job concerning any wrongdoing he may have committed. However, I could not understand why the Lord brought up Job's name to Satan in the first place. For the longest time, I thought God was just trying to brag on Job. *But the real reason is far more redemptive!*

The Lord knew that Satan had a legitimate accusation against Job. (I'll tell you what it is in a second). The only thing that was stopping Satan from ransacking Job's life was the divine hedge of protection God had placed around Job, his family, and possessions. God's divine restraining order prevented Satan from punishing Job for this one flaw in his righteous armor. What was the one "flaw?" Even though Job loved and feared God, he had a major idol in his life! You might find yourself saying, "What? Job had an idol?" Indeed, he did, and I was just as amazed when the Spirit of God showed it to me. In fact, when I saw it, I learned a precious lesson; even the most godly men can have idols!

> *His sons used to go [in turn] and feast in the house of each one on his day, and they would send word and invite their three sisters to eat and drink with them. [5] When the days of their feasting were over, Job would send [for them] and consecrate them, rising early in the morning and offering burnt offerings according to the number of them all; for Job said, "It may be that my sons have sinned and [c]cursed God in their hearts." Job did this at all [such] times.*

Job 1:4-5 (AMP)

So, what was the "idol" in Job's life that caused him to lose all of the riches he had accumulated? His children! Job idolized them, and it cost him dearly! When the Holy Spirit showed it to me, I was speechless! The above passage of scripture from the book of Job brings us face-to-face with how Job idolized his children. Even though He knew God intimately and what God required of His servants, Job never transferred that knowledge to his children. They did not walk in the fear of the Lord and did not seem to care for the Lord at all. In fact, there is not even a single recorded prayer to God from any of Job's children. Thus, they were essentially agnostics.

Even more interesting is that Job never disciplined his children for their worldly and lustful lifestyles. The Bible tells us that Job's children loved to party- every weekend! Everyone in the community knew that if you wanted to get drunk on the weekend, you hooked yourself to Job's children. Apparently, these parties were so wild and reckless that when these blowouts ended, Job rushed to the altar of the Lord to make an atonement for his children – just to cover all their wrongdoing for one weekend!

Listen to Job describe his children after one of their weekend bashes, *"for Job said, "It may be that my sons have sinned and cursed God in their hearts."* What kind of children were these that their godly father was worried that during their drinking and carousing, they might have cursed God? Wow, even when I was a heathen, I had more of the fear of the Lord than Job's children. Unfortunately, because Job made his children into his idols, without knowing it, he had built "evil altars" in his soul upon which he worshipped each one of them! Remember, altars are places of worship. What is worshipped on the altar is the "idol," and every idol is a demon spirit. Parents beware, *loving your children is one thing, but idolizing them leaves you exposed to Satan's influence.*

Most importantly, Job's children did to him what all idols and evil altars do to their human attendants – ***they cost him a fortune!*** While Job's children cared nothing about God, they loved to spend his money and lots of it! All their weekly, lavish and reckless parties were charged to Job's expense account! I believe the reason God brought up Job's name when Satan came to court was that Job had turned his children into idols and let them blow away his fortune!

So, Satan was quick to remind God that the only thing standing between Job and the punishment he deserved for violating the first commandment, "thou shall have no other gods before me," was the "hedge" around him. Satan moved on the Court (God) to remove the restraining order. Once it was removed, Satan quickly pounced on Job. *He stole all of his money, killed all of his servants, and then killed all of Job's idols- his children!* Before the Lord gave me this revelation, I was shocked that the Lord allowed Satan to slaughter all of Job's offspring! However, the Spirit of God told me it was because Job turned his children into idols: God never protects our idols! He judges them! Little did Job realize that he had allowed Satan to use his children to plant a *money-stealing altar* in his life and bloodline. Even though Job was the richest man in the East, Satan always knew he could plunder Job's wealth through his idolatrous connection to his children. *The moral of this story is that hosting idols and evil altars can cost you everything*

Impoverished by Idols!

But the Israelites did evil in the sight of the Lord, and the Lord gave them into the hand of Midian for seven years. ² And the hand of Midian prevailed against Israel. Because of Midian the Israelites made themselves the dens which are in the mountains and the caves and the strongholds. 3 For whenever Israel had sown their seed, the Midianites and the Amalekites and the people of the east came up against them. ⁴ They would encamp against them and destroy the crops as far as Gaza and leave no nourishment for Israel, and no ox or sheep or donkey. ⁵ For they came up with their cattle and their tents, and they came like locusts for multitude; both they and their camels could not be counted. So, they wasted the land as they entered it. ⁶ And Israel was greatly impoverished because of the Midianites, and the Israelites cried to the Lord.

Judges 6:2-6

The attacks by the Midianites and the Amalekites against the land of Israel were so fierce, it left God's people impoverished! Whenever the Israelites planted a field, the enemy came in large numbers and wasted the land. These enemies of Israel entered the land, destroying crops and leaving no nourishment for neither man nor beast. The safety and economic condition of the nation were so strained that the Israelites couldn't even live in their own homes. Rather, they were forced to dwell in mountains and caves.

What in the world would give these evil marauding bands the legal right to strip God's land of its riches? The book of Judges tells us that the Israelites did "evil" in the sight of the Lord, so the Lord handed them over into the hand of Midian for seven years. What sins had the people committed? Idolatry, of course, and not only that, but the people had even set up evil altars from which they worshipped the demon gods of the very nations that were assaulting them!

Confronting Altars in Our Bloodline

That night the Lord said to Gideon, Take your father's bull, the second bull seven years old, and pull down the altar of Baal that your father has and cut down the Asherah [symbol of the goddess Asherah] that is beside it; [26] *And build an altar to the Lord your God on top of this stronghold with stones laid in proper order. Then take the second bull and offer a burnt sacrifice with the wood of the Asherah which you shall cut down.*

Judges 6:25-26

Gideon eventually won a spectacular victory against the Midianites. However, I am convinced, from reading the scriptural passage above, that He would have lost the battle if he had not *first* executed God's judgment against the evil altars of his father's house. What is abundantly clear from observing Gideon's life is that we cannot walk away from confronting the evil altars in our ancestral bloodlines. Such an attitude would be wishful thinking on our part. Let's look at the process Gideon went through as he tore down these unholy altars of worship in his bloodline.

Build an Altar to the Lord First

Before Gideon executed God's judgment against his father's evil altars, he first set up an altar dedicated to the Lord. We must never attempt to take on the evil altars of our father's bloodline unless we are standing on a righteous altar. If we do, we will lose the battle of altars! The enemy will eat us for breakfast if we attempt to overthrow his evil altars with the arm of the flesh. It takes an altar to destroy an altar!

> *When Gideon realized [without any doubt] that He was the Angel of the Lord, he declared, "[b]Oh no, Lord God! For now I have seen the Angel of the Lord face to face [and I am doomed]!"* [23] *The Lord said to him, "Peace to you, do not be afraid; you shall not die."* [24]*Then Gideon built an altar there to the Lord and named it The Lord is Peace. To this day it is still in Ophrah, of the Abiezrites...* [26]*That night the Lord said to Gideon, Take your father's bull, the second bull seven years old, and pull down the altar of Baal that your father has and cut down the Asherah [symbol of the goddess Asherah] that is beside it;*

> Judges 6:22-24, 26 AMP

Gideon immediately erected a righteous altar dedicated to God when the angel of the Lord visited him. Only after this righteous altar was established in his life did he then proceeded to tear down the evil altars his father had erected. Why is this important to note? The Lord told me that the erection of a righteous altar (s) dedicated to the Lord is a critical *first* step in winning the battle of altars and transforming one's life. Standing on a righteous altar that is recognized in the Courts of Heaven is necessary to prosecute and defeat idols and evil altars successfully. My friend Katie Souza told me that she and her staff spent over 40 days building an altar to the Lord through prayer and fasting *before* they then tore down the altars in their family bloodline!

However, as we see in Gideon's life, erecting a righteous altar to the Lord is not the only step required to secure our God-given destiny. The second equally critical step is to tear down our ancestral altars so we can have victory over demonic powers, territorial spirits, as well as ancestral (familiar) spirits. That's what God told Gideon to do, *"Take your father's bull, the second bull seven years old, and pull down the altar of Baal that your father has and cut down the Asherah [symbol of the goddess Asherah] that is beside it."* Notice that when God finished stating His instruction, Gideon was visibly shaken, and a spirit of intimidation tried to get the best of him. God told him to pull down those altars during the day, but he was so frightened he did it at night with ten of his servants. Why was Gideon so intimidated by the thought of destroying the altars of his father's house? Here is the answer the Spirit of God gave me about this. *"Francis, his father's altar, housed the most powerful demons of that time, Baal and Asherah. And since Gideon's father established those altars, that meant those demons had great influence over Gideon himself. They were the most powerful evil altars in Gideon's life because his father established them.*

The Holy Spirit's answer impacted me deeply because it quickly explained the long and fierce spiritual battle I had against the altars of my father's house. I realized too that when our forefathers worship idols and erect evil altars to them, they give authority and permission to these demonic entities to control the second generation. *Bloodline altars are the most difficult ones to overthrow because we have a lot of "things-in-common" with them.* In some cases, we are born carrying these idols and evil altars in our DNA. They can control every part of our physical, mental, and emotional makeup. I am certain that at one-point, Gideon, under the leadership and influence of his father, went to worship at the altar of Baal and Asherah. Thus, those demons were controlling his life.

What is of note is that the two gods the Midianites worshipped were also Baal and Asherah. The Midianites were moon-worshippers. Asherah was the goddess behind this worship of the moon. So how could Gideon destroy the Midianites if he had something in common with their gods? This is why Gideon had to prosecute (pull down) the evil altar of his father's house first, or his attempt to defeat Midian would have ended in disaster. So, the Courts of Heaven issued a judgment against the evil altar of his father's house, and Gideon, as an officer of the Court (remember Gideon was a Judge of Israel), was instructed by God to execute judgment on the altars of Baal and Asherah here on earth.

Impoverished by Money Altars in the Bloodline

For it was whenever Israel had sown [their seed] that the Midianites would come up with the Amalekites and the people of the east and go up against them. ⁴ So they would camp against them and destroy the crops of the land as far as Gaza, and leave no sustenance in Israel as well as no sheep, ox, or donkey. ⁵ For they would come up with their livestock and their tents, and they would come in as numerous as locusts; both they and their camels were innumerable. So, they came into the land to devastate it. ⁶ So Israel was greatly impoverished because of the Midianites, and the Israelites cried out to the Lord [for help].

Judges 6:3-6

The most important thing that I want you to take note of in Gideon's story is just how much the Midianites and Amalekites impoverished Israel. They were placed in such financial despair that they moved themselves from their God-given houses in the promise-land to mountains and

Erecting a righteous altar to God is the first step in winning the battle of the altars.

caves. They did this to hide the little provisions they had left from the Midianites. Gideon was treading wheat in a wine-cellar just to prevent it from being stolen. Why would God let His special people go through such suffering? What's the moral of this story? This is what God showed me: He allowed the Midianites to impoverish the children of Israel to demonstrate that when we worship idols, we automatically give these idols (demon-gods) and the altars they operate from legal rights to control our finances (provisions).

Since the Israelites had abandoned the worship of God and chose to worship Baal and Asherah instead, God allowed the Midianites to plunder Israel's God-given financial fortunes and agricultural resources. This continued until there was almost nothing left. That's when the children of Israel cried to the true God for deliverance, and the Lord chose Gideon to become their judge and deliverer. *But God always delivers the deliverer before He sends him or her to rescue an oppressed people. Gideon had to be delivered first from bowing his knees at the evil altars of Baal and Asherah.*

Judging Evil Altars Breaks the Hold on Your Finances

As soon as Gideon obeyed the Lord and pulled down the evil altars of his father's house, a huge demonic pandemonium ensued, but then Gideon also experienced a massive financial breakthrough! First, when his father's idolatrous parishioners discovered that the evil altars that hosted Baal and the goddess Asherah had been torn down, they went into a violent riot (much like the people of Ephesus). They wanted to kill Gideon. But interestingly enough, it was his father who was a priest to Baal and Asherah, who came to his son's defense. This was the first proof that the evil altar of his father's house had been judged and destroyed.

Then, immediately after this, Gideon moved into a season of unprecedented breakthrough, right up to his glorious victory over the Midianites with only 300 hundred men!

Then Zebah and Zalmunna said, Rise yourself and fall on us; for as the man is, so is his strength. And Gideon arose and slew Zebah and Zalmunna and took the [crescent-shaped] ornaments that were on their camels' necks.

Judges 8:21 AMPC

Once Gideon brought judgment on the altars his father built, he was not only able to defeat the Ammonites and Midianites but also broke the stronghold on his finances! God gave Gideon supernatural grace to kill two Midian army generals by the names of Zebah and Zalmunna. After which, Gideon took from those kings the *crescent-shaped ornaments that were on their camels' necks*. These *crescent-shaped ornaments* were the most expensive pieces of jewelry the Midianites had, that's why they decorated their two top generals with them. Now they were in Gideon's possession! The spirit of poverty over Gideon's life was finally broken.

It's also interesting to note that those ornaments Gideon took were *"crescent-shaped ornaments."* This is prophetically significant because the worship of the goddess Asherah was represented by a crescent moon, the same crescent moon that you see today in the Muslim faith. God giving these priceless ornaments of the Midianites to Gideon was a prophetic statement that the idolatry to Baal and Asherah that had brought the Israelites into bondage was utterly broken.

Explosive Financial Breakthrough!

Then the men of Israel said to Gideon, Rule over us—you and your son and your son's son also—for you have delivered us from the hand of Midian. [23] And Gideon said to them, "I will not rule over you, and my son will not rule over you; the Lord will rule over you." [24] And Gideon said to them, "Let me make a request of you—every man of you give me the earrings of his spoil." For [the Midianites] had gold earrings because they were Ishmaelites [general term for all descendants of Keturah]. [25] And they answered, "We will willingly give them." And they spread a garment, and every man cast on it the earrings of his spoil. 26 And the weight of the golden earrings that he requested was 1,700 shekels of gold, besides the crescents and pendants and the purple garments worn by the kings of Midian, and the chains that were about their camels' necks.

Judges 8:22-26, AMPC

After destroying the evil altars of his father's house and defeating the Midianites in battle, Gideon entered into a season of explosive financial breakthrough. Gideon's men were so overwhelmed by how God used him to deliver the nation from the Midianites; they begged him to become king. However, Gideon knew that God did not want him to be their king. God was going to rule His people.

However, Gideon asked his men to do him one favor. The Bible records, *"Gideon said to them, let me make a request of you—every man of you give me the earrings of his spoil."* These earrings were made of pure gold. The Midian army was in the hundreds of thousands, and each soldier had these golden earrings. When Gideon's men surrendered each of their spoil of earrings, there were heaps and heaps of them. Do the math! Gideon and his descendants never lacked money ever again! This is what God is going to do for you and me when we renounce idolatry and prosecute every evil altar in our bloodline. I know this firsthand! I love the Lord dearly, but for years I struggled financially until recently. I am now living in an endless season of financial breakthrough.

Do you want to know how it happened? Let me tell you!

The Prophetic Dream that Changed My Family!

[One may hear God's voice] in a dream, in a vision of the night, when deep sleep falls on men while slumbering upon the bed, [16] Then He opens the ears of men and seals their

---

instruction [terrifying them with warnings], ¹⁷ That He may withdraw man from his purpose and cut off pride from him [disgusting him with his own disappointing self-sufficiency]. ¹⁸ He holds him back from the pit [of destruction], and his life from perishing by the sword [of God's destructive judgments].

Job 33:15-18

I have seen the precepts in the story of Gideon manifest in my own life. Once, I, too, destroyed the evil altars in my bloodline, and I experienced a massive breakthrough in my finances! My dear mother, Ester, died and went to be with Jesus in May of 2015, and my father followed her to heaven a year later. She was my best friend, and I mourned her deeply. I mention her heavenly transition only to give you context concerning the prophetic dream God gave my sister Judith in 2018, that changed everything for our family and the projection of my ministry! I will let my sister Judy tell it in her own words.

"I greet you all in Jesus' name. My beloved ones, this is a dream I had after reading the book Issuing Divine Restraining Orders from the Courts of Heaven, by Dr. Francis Myles. In my dream, I found myself in Ndola, standing near our family house. I was wondering what I was doing there. Suddenly I saw a woman running towards me. She was telling me something I couldn't understand. As I was trying to catch what she was saying, I heard a voice behind me. It was Mum's voice. She told me not to listen to the other woman. Mum then gave me an old thick book, which had old dirty pages. She told me to burn the book. "This is the book that contains all the bad things that were spoken over our family." Mum declared. She then told me to extend my right hand, which I did. She handed me a green, new book. It looked like a diary. She said to me, "this book is where all the good things God intended for our family are written."

When I lifted up my face, I found myself inside our Ndola family house inside the girls' bedroom. I heard a knock on the window. When I opened it, Emmanuel (my brother) was telling me to open the door for him. I went out of the bedroom to the sitting room, where I found a lot of Dad's relatives sleeping. I was very upset, and I said to myself, "why don't you leave us alone? Even when Dad has died, you are still following us." When I reached the kitchen, the door leading to the backyard looked old, as if it had been closed for a long time. Mother appeared again in my dream and gave me the keys to open the ancient-looking kitchen door. "Open it!" Mum declared. When I opened the kitchen door, I saw that there was a shrine (an altar) in the backyard. I screamed in anger! I found myself saying, "who built this altar? It must be destroyed!" I was shouting in my dream; then I woke up. The dream bothered me deeply. I asked the Holy Spirit, "what is this?" The Spirit said, "remember that it is in Ndola where your father lost everything he owned. It is also where all of you, as a family unit, got scattered into different cities. That was the beginning of your downfall!"

Ladies and gentlemen, when my dear sister Judy posted this prophetic dream on our family WhatsApp group, my spirit exploded into action. I was in America at my home in Scottsdale, Arizona. The Holy Spirit told me to come before the altar of the LORD in my home. At the time, the Spirit of God had been teaching me on the subject of altars. As soon as I knelt in prayer, the Spirit of God spoke to me. "Son, do you want to know the name of the evil altar of your father's house that you have been fighting for years?" I said, "Yes, Lord," as I was desperate for answers! "It's called the altar that scatters in Ndola. This is the demonic altar that has scattered many of your divine relationships, churches, businesses, open-doors, and financial opportunities that I have tried to bless you with." I was stunned, speechless. At the same time, a sense of pure relief went over me. *The mystery of my struggles in life had just been revealed. I was no longer shadow boxing a mysterious enemy.*

Seizing the Horns of Destiny!

But the Spirit of the Lord clothed Gideon with Himself and took possession of him, and he blew a trumpet, and [the clan of] Abiezer was gathered to him.

Judges 6:34

"I want you to fly to Zambia with your wife and take Judy and several of your blood brothers and travel to your old house in Ndola. Go and pull down the altar of your father's house, and everything I have been trying to give you will stay with you permanently." Even though the last time I traveled to Ndola was over 28 years ago, I did not hesitate in my obedience. When my wife and I landed in Lusaka, Zambia, we rented a truck and drove with six members of my family to our old house in the city of Ndola. When we arrived, I went to the backyard to the exact spot my sister was shown in her prophetic dream. We repented, prayed, and did a prophetic act of tearing down the evil altar of our father's house. We took both the idol and evil altar to the Courts of Heaven and prosecuted them.

The Spirit of God told me that it was done! The righteous judge had just handed down a righteous verdict of release and deliverance. I even asked the Lord, the righteous judge, for punitive damages against the idol and evil altar of my father's house for all the spiritual, emotional, and financial losses my family had suffered for generations. Since then, my wife and I have experienced exponential growth in our ministry in the USA and around the world. Doors of ministry and television (which were closed for years) suddenly swung wide open! I was even offered a fully paid global television ministry on a major TV network!

Since we pulled down and prosecuted the evil altar of my father's house, our ministry has been flooded with people wanting to donate to our ministry. My personal and ministry account balances are showing figures I had only previously dreamed of. My wife and I went from not owning any land to owning over 300 acres of farming land and a fully operational farm, within six months of pulling down the evil altar and idol of my father's house! There is nothing we have done differently in the natural to merit what's taking place in our life and ministry, except for the act of tearing down the evil altar of the idol of my father's house. Please remember, God is no respecter of persons. He will do the same thing for you too! It's your time! (FYI: *You don't have to go to an actual physical location to tear down the altar of your father's house, that is just what the Holy Spirit required of me. You can prosecute and tear down the evil altar and idol of your father's house from the comfort of your home or office if you simply come into the Courts of Heaven.*)

God is no respecter of
persons. He will do the
same thing for you.
IT'S YOUR TIME!

Life Application Section

Memory Verse

That night the Lord said to Gideon, Take your father's bull, the second bull seven years old, and pull down the altar of Baal that your father has and cut down the Asherah [symbol of the goddess Asherah] that is beside it; [26] *And build an altar to the Lord your God on top of this stronghold with stones laid in proper order. Then take the second bull and offer a burnt sacrifice with the wood of the Asherah which you shall cut down.* Judges 6:25-26

Reflections

1. What kind of spoils of war did Gideon ask him men to give him?

_____

_____

_____

_____

2. Why did God tell Gideon to tear down the altar of Baal that his father erected?

_____

_____

_____

_____

_____

_____

Prayer of Release #8

Prosecuting Money Stealing Altars

"Heavenly Father, I ask for the Court of Heaven to be seated, as I come before the judge of all the earth to plead my case so I can be justified and delivered from the evil altars of my father's house. I am here in court with my official representative, the Holy Spirit, my advocate and counselor. Heavenly Father, I surrender all rights to self-representation; instead, I summon my defense attorney and mediator of the New Covenant, the Lord Jesus Christ, to represent me in your Royal Courtroom. Heavenly Father, I am in your Supreme Court to prosecute all idols and evil altars controlling my life and bloodline, in Jesus' Name. Heavenly Father, Satan can no longer retain any legal rights to deny my destiny from manifesting in the earth.

I now enter a plea of 'guilty' into the court's records concerning setting up evil altars in my bloodline. The Bible says in Matthew 5:25, *Come to terms quickly [at the earliest opportunity] with your opponent at law while you are with him on the way [to court], so that your opponent does not hand you over to the judge, and the judge to the guard, and you are thrown into prison."*

Righteous Judge, since I am under oath, I cannot lie about my sinful activities and transgressions connected to my idolatry. I agree with any legitimate accusations brought against me and my ancestral bloodline by Satan. I submit a plea of guilty to all of Satan's charges connected to any idolatry that my ancestors or I committed. I now formally submit my guilty plea to the court in Jesus' Name. *And they overcame him by the blood of the Lamb and by the word of their testimony, and they did not love their lives to the death.* Revelation 12:11 (NKJV)

As I am now called to testify on the witness stand, I humbly repent of all the charges leveled against me so that I can overcome the enemy through the power of the blood and the word of my testimony. I repent of all sin connected to setting up evil money stealing altars. I repent on behalf of my forefathers who established these evil, money-stealing altars. I will not allow myself or my finances to be controlled by these evil, money stealing altars. I repent for spending money on them and coming into partnership and fellowship with them.

I repent for spending money on idols so my soul could find temporary comfort. I repent for buying the useless, powerless products crafted by the Demetriuses of this world. I repent for all the financial altars that were established in my bloodline. I repent for making my children into idols like Job did and letting them recklessly spend my money and not correcting them. I repent for setting up altars to Baal, and Asherah like Gideon's father did. I plead with the court to put my sin under the blood of Jesus so I can overcome the accuser through my redeemers' blood. In Jesus' Name, Amen.

As I continue to testify in this court, I also decree that I am under the power of the free and unmerited Grace of God. Since the Bible says it's impossible to keep the whole law, I need the grace of the Lord Jesus Christ. I admit to this court that my sins of idolatry, bowing to evil altars, and spending my money on these evil altars have increased and abounded. I now decree Grace has increased even the more over my sin and even superabounded. I also decree Psalms 118:27 over myself.

The LORD is God, and He has given us light [illuminating us with His grace and freedom and joy]. Bind the festival sacrifices with [cords to the horns of the altar.

Heavenly Father, Righteous Judge, I decree that because of the blood of Jesus and the power of His grace, my bloodline and I must be acquitted of all charges of erecting evil money stealing altars in our bloodline. Heavenly Father, I request that You go back to the first time my ancestors erected these evil altars to their lifeless idols and then judge these evil, money stealing altars. Righteous Judge, I ask you to use Your judicial discretion to reverse every generational and financial curse over my life." In Jesus' Name. Amen

Now, Invite Jesus To Heal Your Soul!

Holy Spirit, I now invite you to search my soul (my will, mind, and emotions) and judge every idol and evil altar in my life and bloodline that is connected to my finances. The Bible says in 3 John 2 that I will prosper even as my soul prospers. Lord Jesus, I am asking You to cleanse my soul with Your blood, so that every wound in my soul connected to my finances can be cleansed. The Bible says it's the blood that atones for the soul. The Bible also declares that the blood cleanses my conscience; thus, I decree the blood is cleansing my mind right now of all thoughts connected to money that would shipwreck my finances. I decree the blood is cleansing my will so that it won't be controlled by evil, money stealing altars that drive me to make bad decisions with my finances. I declare the blood is also cleansing my emotions to sever them from the control of idols and evil altars that drive me to make emotional purchases.

Lord Jesus, I am asking You to also use your "Dunamis Power" according to Acts 10:38 to heal every wound in my soul that any evil money stealing altar is using to rob me, put poverty on me, and to attack me financially. I also decree Ephesians 3:16 over myself that my soul is being strengthened and re-enforced by mighty Dunamis Power through the Holy Spirit. Thus, I am being strengthened in my soul to resist spending my money lavishly and recklessly. These money stealing altars will not direct my thoughts, emotions, or my will anymore. Finally, I decree and declare that I am full of the light of Christ. As John 8:12 says, *"Once more Jesus addressed the crowd. He said, "I am the Light of the world. He who follows Me will not walk in the darkness but will have the Light of life."* I decree my soul is not walking in darkness, and I have the light, which is life, so my finances will also be full of life.

Loudly Declare These Supernatural Decrees So You Can Have Your Breakthrough

Heavenly Father

- I decree and declare that the influence and power of the Midianites and Amalekites over my finances is broken over my life

- I decree and declare that you are restoring all my lost fortunes as you did with Job after you delivered him of idols and evil altars in his bloodline

- I decree and declare that every evil altar of my father's house, which was stealing my finances, is permanently judged in Jesus' Name.

- I decree and declare that just like Job, you are giving me more than I lost to the money stealing evil altars of my father's house.

- I decree and declare that every idol and evil altar in my bloodline is destroyed in Jesus' Name

- I decree and declare that just as you changed Gideon's financial fortunes and gave him the grace to plunder the Midianites of all their wealth, I receive the same grace and power in Jesus' Name.

- I decree and declare that my finances are entering into a season of explosive growth in Jesus' Name.

- I decree and declare that as I bring my sacrificial offering into the Courts of Heaven, the power of evil altars over my finances is permanently destroyed. In Jesus' Name. Amen

Time to Take Communion

Lord, as I take this communion, I do it in remembrance of You and Your victory on the cross and the resurrection. I decree that as I drink this cup of Your blood and eat Your body, my sins are forgiven, and my soul is nourished and refreshed and strengthened. I decree that as I eat Your flesh and drink Your blood, I will never be hungry and thirsty for idols again. I decree that as I partake of Your supper that my "Not Guilty" verdict from this Court concerning "Setting up evil altars in my life and bloodline," will be sealed by the power and testimony of Your body and blood in Jesus' Name.

THE IDOLS ARE RIOTING

About The Authors

Dr. Francis Myles

In 1989, near the point of death, Dr. Myles had a divine encounter with Jesus Christ Himself. After this powerful healing encounter, Dr. Myles was anointed with a strong gift of healing and prophecy. As a result, he has seen thousands of people healed through his crusades and meetings.

Known as a great "revelator." Dr. Myles has been gifted with biblical insight and revelation into many hidden mysteries of the Word. He is most well-known for his revelation of the Order of Melchizedek. This revelation has resulted in the creation of "The Order of Melchizedek Supernatural School of Ministry," where he has graduated thousands of students worldwide who have learned the lifechanging principles of living as "kings and priests" under this powerful Order.

Dr. Myles is a world-renowned author of many life-changing books such as *The Order of Melchizedek, Issuing Divine Restraining Orders from the Courts of Heaven,* and *The Joseph of Arimethea Calling,* to name just a few. He has made several appearances on TBN, GodTV, and Daystar Christian TV networks. He has been a featured guest on Sid Roth's "Its Supernatural TV show, and This Is Your Day with Benny Hinn."

Dr. Francis Myles is also the founder of Marketplace Bible™ International, the creator of the world's first digital Marketplace Bible, which is designed to help millions of Christians around the world to "apply timeless biblical principles to today's marketplace." He is happily married to the love of his life, Carmela Real Myles. Together they reside in McDonough, Georgia, a suburb of Atlanta.

Katie Souza

Katie was a career criminal most of her life, was convicted of several felonies and sent to federal prison to serve almost twelve years. While serving what would be her final prison sentence, Katie encountered God in a way that dramatically changed her life. She immediately became an outspoken advocate for Jesus, and her infectious love for Him caused many women inside her cell block to accept Him as their Savior.

Katie launched *Healing Your Soul; Real Keys to the Miraculous* in the fall of 2013 on just a few television networks. Today, the program is broadcast weekly on airwaves around the world. It has developed a faithful following of people who are eager for the supernatural in their lives and the blessed transformation of a healthy soul. All of the television shows are available for viewing at any time, on her website katiesouza.com, absolutely free of charge! Katie lives in Arizona with her husband, Robert, and their three small dogs. She writes, teaches, produces a television show which is broadcast around the world, and travels extensively. Katie and Robert visit prisons several times each year to teach inmates how to hear from God and to demonstrate that they too can achieve what God has promised and planned for them. She continues in full pursuit of her expected end.

Endnotes

Chapter 1

[i] https://www.statista.com/statistics/1109183/alcoholic-beverages-sales-growth-coronavirus-us/

[ii] https://www.statista.com/statistics/1109183/alcoholic-beverages-sales-growth-coronavirus-us/

Made in the USA
Coppell, TX
10 March 2024

29948578R00127